BETTER

COACHING OURSELVES AND EACH OTHER
TO BE MORE CREDIBLE, CARING, AND CONNECTED

CONVERSATIONS

What Your Colleagues Are Saying . . .

"I thought I knew how to have a conversation; I've had millions of them. Some were good, others not so much so. But I want to have GREAT conversations, and Jim Knight has taught me how. The proof is in: better conversations are possible, and the results are worth the investment."

—DOUGLAS FISHER
Coauthor of *Rigorous Reading* and *Unstoppable Learning*

"*Better Conversations* stimulates the mind, spirit, and soul of those who coach, regardless of their role or position, by unpacking and reshaping the mental models that drive how they think, speak, and act . . . I found myself frequently thinking about how helpful this book will be to nearly every human who interacts with others, whether in school or beyond."

—JOELLEN KILLION
Senior Advisor, Learning Forward

"I read more education books than I care to admit. Some are good, some are bad, and very few are great. Jim Knight's book *Better Conversations* is BRILLIANT! *Insightful, innovative,* and *practical* are the three words that kept coming to me when I was reading and learning from his book. Jim treats the subject of communication as an art and gives all of us, regardless of position or years of experience, practical ways to use our voice to improve the teaching and learning environment, as well as ourselves!"

—RUSSELL J. QUAGLIA
President/Founder
Quaglia Institute for Student Aspirations

"*Better Conversations* is just what the title says. Jim Knight moves learning conversations ahead for educators to deepen trust, meaning, and actions. He summarizes current thinking from multiple authors that will make learning for adults and students better. Activities at the end of each chapter can be used for self-reflection, team learning, and schoolwide focus on learning. The vignettes are real issues in schools, which makes this book very important for our profession."

—WILLIAM SOMMERS
Retired Principal and Leadership Coach
Austin, Texas

JIM KNIGHT

BETTER
COACHING OURSELVES AND EACH OTHER
TO BE MORE CREDIBLE, CARING, AND CONNECTED
CONVERSATIONS

CORWIN
A SAGE Company

FOR INFORMATION:

Corwin
A SAGE Company
2455 Teller Road
Thousand Oaks, California 91320
(800) 233-9936
www.corwin.com

SAGE Publications Ltd.
1 Oliver's Yard
55 City Road
London EC1Y 1SP
United Kingdom

SAGE Publications India Pvt. Ltd.
B 1/I 1 Mohan Cooperative Industrial Area
Mathura Road, New Delhi 110 044
India

SAGE Publications Asia-Pacific Pte. Ltd.
3 Church Street
#10-04 Samsung Hub
Singapore 049483

Program Director: Dan Alpert
Senior Associate Editor: Kimberly Greenberg
Editorial Assistant: Katie Crilley
Production Editor: Melanie Birdsall
Copy Editor: Lana Todorovic-Arndt
Typesetter: C&M Digitals (P) Ltd.
Proofreader: Theresa Kay
Indexer: Sylvia Coates
Graphic Designer: Alexa Turner
Marketing Manager: Maura Sullivan

Cover design by Clinton Carlson.

Printed in the United States of America

ISBN 978-1-5063-0745-9

Library of Congress Control Number: 2015949335

This book is printed on acid-free paper.

Certified Chain of Custody
Promoting Sustainable Forestry
www.sfiprogram.org
SFI-01268

SFI label applies to text stock

18 19 10 9 8 7 6

CONTENTS

Visit the companion website at
**http://resources.corwin.com/
KnightBetterConversations**
for downloadable resources.

This book is dedicated to David Knight, my son, who, I'm extremely proud to say, is hard at work making a difference by studying coaching, cost effectiveness of professional development, and other issues critical to helping schools make a difference for children.

Now you're my mentor, Dave. I'm grateful for all you teach me, and I am especially proud to see how you have grown to be a man who beautifully embodies the beliefs and habits described in this book.

PREFACE

At a recent concert, I heard Andy Gullahorn sing a song that I happen to like quite a bit, "I Will." In the song, he tells his friends the ways in which he will be a committed friend to them. When he introduced the song at the concert, Andy said, "I didn't write this song because this is the kind of person I am. I wrote this song because this is the kind of person I want to be."

I've written this book with the same thought in mind. I acquired the ideas in this book from hundreds of people who participated in our study of communication in schools. I also learned the ideas from many wise people who've written important books about communication. And I love presenting this material to audiences because each presentation reminds me to do the simple things I often forget to do: listen, pay attention, care, seek out the things I hold in common with others, demonstrate empathy, and be a witness to what is good. Like Andy Gullahorn, I didn't write this book because this is the kind of person I am. I wrote the book to describe the person I want to be. I also wrote it because I believe most people who read this will feel the same. We all want to be better, and we fall short. I wanted to write something that honestly acknowledged our own difficulties with communication but that also offered a pathway forward.

This book comes from several sources. First, many of the ideas were included in chapters in other books I've written, in particular Chapter 4 in *Instructional Coaching* (2007) and Chapter 7 in *Unmistakable Impact* (2011). If you have read those books (and thank you very much if you have), you will see some ideas and words or sentences here that you have seen before. In part, I wrote this book to gather all I've written and said about communication in the past and then expand it. So, I've gone back to the older books and added those ideas here.

This book also draws on the work of wise and insightful authors whose books on communication are packed with excellent advice on how to listen, build relationships, encourage others, control our emotions, share ideas, and do many other aspects of communication. My life is better because of the books I reference throughout this book.

In large measure, this book is based on all I learned from educators who applied the self-coaching strategies described in this book. To test out my central idea—that we can coach ourselves to improve our communication skills—I had the help of approximately 200 volunteers from around the world (Canada, United States, Mexico, India, Australia, Dubai, and Thailand). These individuals tried out the communication habits in their schools or homes and then shared their completed self-coaching forms with my colleagues and me at the Impact Research Lab.

Each volunteer attempted to learn and adopt at least one of the Better Conversations Habits described in this book; some of those volunteers tried several. To do this, they read descriptions of the habits and then decided how they would try to put those habits into practice in a future conversation. Following this, they would usually video record that conversation and then analyze their video using the reflection forms at the end of each chapter. Often volunteers continued to practice the habits until they felt they had mastered them, and some adopted several habits.

Once volunteers completed experimenting with the habit they had been given, they filled out surveys describing their experiences. They then sent their surveys along with their completed reflection forms to the Impact Research Lab. In total, my colleagues and I reviewed more than 1,000 reflection forms. The volunteers' comments helped me refine the forms and the learning process. More important, perhaps, the written comments we received tangibly demonstrated that each of us can learn to have better conversations. Each reflection form paints a picture of how each person did just that.

The experience that many people around the world have had—coaching themselves to improve the way they communicate—is an experience you can and—dare I say it?—should have. This book explains how you can coach yourself to have better conversations, and I include many of the stories of people who made real, unmistakable improvements in the way they communicate. When possible, I include the names of the volunteers who tried out the Better Conversations Habits. On some occasions, however, I change the names and some details about people to ensure that confidentiality is respected. I also change the wording of some comments slightly to increase coherence or clarity. All quotations were reviewed by volunteers to ensure that the meaning correctly reflected their views.

You may use this book in many different ways. First, you may want to use it on your own to video or audio record your conversations in school or home, to set communication goals, and to monitor your progress toward your goals until they are met. You may wish to share video recordings of your conversations with friends or colleagues and collaborate with them to explore, plan, and implement communication habits that help all of you improve. Additionally, coaches may wish to use the habits and self-coaching forms to coach people who are intent on improving their communication skills. Teams of teachers, coaches, administrators, or others may wish to learn together. Indeed, whole schools or districts might commit to implement the Better Conversations Habits.

This process pushed me to video record myself in the same way that I ask others to engage in video protocols with the purpose of deeper understanding. Reflecting on my experiences felt like a gift I gave myself. I actually savored the time and experience of answering questions and considering my strengths as well as areas in which I can grow.

—Michelle Murray,
Instructional Coach,
Anacortes, Washington

ACKNOWLEDGMENTS

Every book involves the efforts of many more people than the author, but this one, without question, involved the largest team ever. I am profoundly grateful to all the people who helped me make this book a reality.

More than anyone else, I'm grateful to my wife Jenny, who has been my greatest support as I wrote this book. Jenny has tirelessly read every word multiple times, given me great feedback, put together many sections of the book, helped with the design of the forms, reviewed each copy edit and done her own copy editing, and been a wonderful partner throughout the whole process—even putting up with the many times when I have failed at the habits I'm describing. I love you more than anything, Jen. You're my favorite conversation partner, and I've loved putting this book together with you.

I'm grateful to my parents Joan and Doug Knight, who engendered in me a love of learning that is still alive and flourishing today.

My deep thanks to my children Geoff, Cameron, David, Emily, Ben, Isaiah, and Luke; thank you for sticking with me as I've failed again and again at the strategies I describe in this book. You amaze me and fill me with pride when I see the good work you are doing around the world.

At the Impact Research Lab, many consultants have helped immensely. Carol Hatton organized the first study in 2010 and helped with the 2015 study all while doing a million others tasks for me. Devona Dunekack organized, gathered, and analyzed data from the 2015 study; often created surveys; helped design forms; and reviewed the 1,000 plus reflection forms we gathered for this project. Marilyn Ruggles analyzed and organized data, reviewed books and literature, conducted interviews, and did transcriptions and many other tasks to help me create this book. On very short notice, Jackie Schafer and Stacey Blakeman edited this book and made it much easier for you to read. Kirsten McBride, who has improved every book I have written, proofread the text with great care. I am also grateful to Clinton Carlson, who created the cover for this book. Clint, I am always amazed by your talent.

At the Instructional Coaching Group, Ruth Ryschon and Brooke Deaton have ensured that the consulting work we do goes off without a hitch.

My friends at Corwin have been incredibly helpful. Dan Alpert has been my editor for close to a decade, and I'm profoundly grateful for his wisdom, patience, insight, and feedback. Melanie Birdsall is a wonderful professional who does amazing work and does it while making me feel deeply encouraged. I'm also very grateful to my many additional Corwin partners, Mike Soules, Kristin Anderson, Mayan McDermott, Stephanie Trkay, Monique Corridori, and Taryn Williams.

At the Kansas University Center for Research on Learning, I'm very grateful to Center Director Mike Hock, my colleagues Irma Brasseur-Hock and Jan Bulgren, and my mentors Don Deshler, Marti Elford, and Jean Schumaker.

Finally, I can't even begin to say how deeply grateful I am to the many people who participated in our global study of the Better Conversations Habits and Beliefs. Approximately 200 people from around the world spent hours and hours watching themselves on video, completing the reflection forms, and communicating with our team. Your stories touched me, inspired me, and made it clear to me that trying to have better conversations is a worthwhile endeavor. I've tried to list all of the volunteers at the end of this book.

Finally, I wrote most of this book listening to Miles Davis and Bill Evans, and especially Miles Davis' recordings with his first great quartet on the Prestige Albums he recorded over a weekend in May 1956 and Bill Evans' breathtakingly beautiful *Complete Live at the Village Vanguard*, which has now become my favorite album to listen to while I write.

Publisher's Acknowledgments

Corwin gratefully acknowledges the contributions of the following contributors:

Lydia Adegbola
Assistant Principal
Legacy School for
   Integrated Studies
New York, NY

Ruthanne Bolling
Instructional Coach
Fairview Elementary,
   Richmond
   Community Schools
Richmond, IN

Dr. Alison Gordon
Instructor, School
   of Education
Northwestern
   University
Evanston, IL

Kathryn Kee
Educational Leader;
   Owner of Results
   Coaching, LLC
Shady Shores, TX

Ellen Larsen
Manager (Teaching
   and Learning)
Independent Schools
   Queensland
Brisbane, Australia

Dr. William Sommers
Retired Principal,
   Leadership Coach,
   Author
Spring Lake Park District
Spring Lake Park, MN

Susan K. Woodruff
Professional Developer and
   Instructional Coach
KUCRL & Strategic
   Consulting
Muskegon, MI

ABOUT THE AUTHOR

 **Jim Knight** has spent more than two decades studying professional learning, effective teaching, and instructional coaching. He is a research associate at the University of Kansas Center for Research on Learning and the president of the Instructional Coaching Group and the Impact Research Lab.

Jim's book *Instructional Coaching: A Partnership Approach to Improving Instruction* (Corwin, 2007) popularized the idea of instructional coaching. Jim edited *Coaching: Approaches and Perspectives* (Corwin, 2009) and coauthored *Coaching Classroom Management* (Pacific Northwest Publishing, 2010). Jim's other books include *Unmistakable Impact: A Partnership Approach for Dramatically Improving Instruction* (Corwin, 2011), *High-Impact Instruction: A Framework for Great Teaching* (Corwin, 2013), and *Focus on Teaching: Using Video for High-Impact Instruction* (Corwin, 2014).

Jim's articles on professional learning, teaching, and instructional coaching have appeared in journals such as *The Journal of Staff Development*, *Principal Leadership*, *The School Administrator*, *Kappan*, and *Educational Leadership*.

Frequently asked to lead professional learning, Jim has presented to more than 30,000 educators from six continents. He has a PhD in Education from the University of Kansas and has won several university teaching, innovation, and service awards. Jim also writes the Radical Learners blog.

**Better
Conversations**

are about

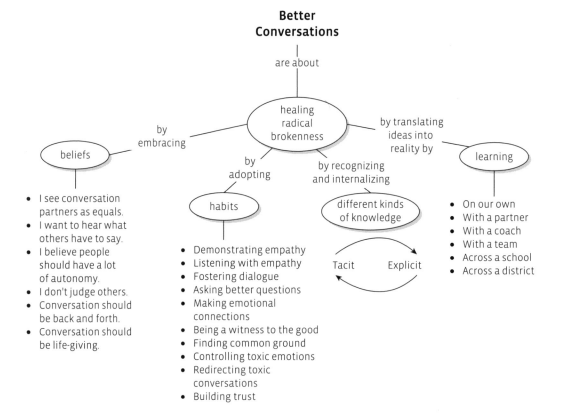

by
embracing

healing
radical
brokenness

by translating
ideas into
reality by

beliefs

by
adopting

by recognizing
and internalizing

learning

- I see conversation
  partners as equals.
- I want to hear what
  others have to say.
- I believe people
  should have a lot
  of autonomy.
- I don't judge others.
- Conversation should
  be back and forth.
- Conversation should
  be life-giving.

habits

different kinds
of knowledge

- On our own
- With a partner
- With a coach
- With a team
- Across a school
- Across a district

Tacit   Explicit

- Demonstrating empathy
- Listening with empathy
- Fostering dialogue
- Asking better questions
- Making emotional
  connections
- Being a witness to the good
- Finding common ground
- Controlling toxic emotions
- Redirecting toxic
  conversations
- Building trust

RADICAL BROKENNESS AND BETTER CONVERSATIONS

I believe we can change the world if we start listening to one another again. Simple, honest, human conversation. Not mediation, negotiation, problem-solving, debate, or public meetings. Simple, truthful conversation where we each have a chance to speak, we each feel heard, and we each listen well.

—Margaret Wheatley (2002, p. 3)

Doing the Better Conversation study, I think I have started to see a better version of myself, and who doesn't want that?

—Ben Collins, Assistant Principal,
Des Plaines, Illinois

Every day I am reminded of the power of better conversations. Some days I am encouraged by what I see and hear. A few years ago, I was talking about empathy with a group of instructional coaches in a school district in the Pacific Northwest, and I gave everyone some homework for the night—to try to put empathy into practice in some concrete way.

The next morning, prior to the workshop, one of the participants, a man in his mid-fifties, walked over to me to talk. Barely holding back his emotions, he told me about his experience the night before, saying something like the following:

> I have to tell you about what we did yesterday—the stuff about empathy. When we talked about that, I thought about my best friend. We got into an argument about five years ago, and we stopped talking. I would drive by his house on my way to work every day, and just seeing his house would make me angry. But yesterday, when we talked about empathy, I realized that I was a part of the problem. I called him last night to apologize. And when I did that, he apologized, too. All the anger is gone. We are back to being friends. It's like the argument never happened.

Stories like this give me hope that we can have better conversations.

Yet, often I am discouraged. Recent data from the National Center for Health Statistics (Copen, Daniels, Vespa, & Mosher, 2012) predict that 40–50% of American marriages will end in divorce, and there are too many marriages that do not end in divorce but are nothing more than marriages in name only. Too often a relationship starts out with joy and hope and sometimes a deep, sacred commitment, only to end with pain, anger, and resentment. Compounding this distressing situation is the fact that our work lives can also be very difficult. I have seen far too many ineffective, painful, even damaging conversations within the walls of our schools. Stories I hear from homes and schools show me why we need better conversations.

What is common to these stories of hope and despair is the reality that communication is terribly important. In schools, better conversations can dramatically improve educator and student learning. When teachers are clearer, ask better questions, and foster dialogue, their students learn more. Similarly, when teachers listen, find common ground, foster trust, and make connections, students feel more psychologically safe. Everyone, adults and children, experiences greater well-being when they are heard, respected, and engaged.

Better conversations also stand at the heart of professional learning in schools. Instructional coaches who learn to be better at listening, questioning, building emotional connections, and fostering dialogue become more effective. Communication is the lifeblood of coaching, and the more effectively coaches communicate, the more effectively everyone learns.

Communication is also essential for other forms of professional learning. When trust, respect, and clear communication are cultural norms, teachers are more comfortable sharing ideas and learning from each other. Better conversations will improve collaboration, team meetings, professional learning communities, and other conversations about teaching and learning. Better conversations also lead to fewer hard feelings and more listening, respect, kindness, and candor.

Schools should be places where children experience safer, more positive, and better learning because all educators work to improve the way they communicate. For that reason, I believe one of the most important and powerful ways we can improve our schools is to improve the way we interact with each other.

Effective communication is an essential part of our professional lives, but I believe it is even more important in our personal lives. Much of our joy and sorrow is the direct result of our personal relationships, and our relationships thrive or die depending on how well we communicate. When we listen with empathy, find common bonds, and build emotional connections, we find that our lives at home, at work, and in the community are better. Taking time to improve our conversations is probably one of the best ways we can spend our time because so much of our success and happiness hinge on how well we communicate, and because far too frequently we are frustrated or saddened by how our conversations fail.

Margaret Wheatley, author of *Turning to One Another: Simple Conversations to Restore Hope to the Future* (2002), has written about our struggle to communicate. She uses Desmond Tutu's words to describe how we interact with others: "We have never wanted to be alone. But today, we are alone. We are more fragmented and isolated from one another than ever before. Archbishop Desmond Tutu describes it as 'a radical brokenness in all of existence'" (p. 4).

I believe we are "radically broken" as Desmond Tutu says,[1] because although we need to be in relationships, we live in isolation, often even when we live with others in the same building. We are broken though we have more ways to connect than ever before—Facebook, Twitter, Skype, texting, email, Instagram, Pinterest, and so on. Unity is our natural state; isolation is what we experience. Better conversations can help us heal that radical brokenness and restore unity.

I called this book *Better Conversations* for two reasons. First, I describe simple, clear steps we can take to coach ourselves to have better conversations. Meaningful, respectful conversations can build a tie between people that is deep, strong, life-giving, and maybe even lifelong. Better conversations are the glue that holds together the faithful relationships we build our lives around. This book is meant to help us get better at fostering and sustaining such empowering interactions.

I also chose *Better Conversations* as the title to emphasize that healthy conversations and dialogue should leave us feeling better about life and our lives in particular. As Paulo Freire (1970) has written, through authentic, meaningful interaction, we can experience "mutually humanizing conversations." This book is about how we can get better at the kind of conversations that help us be better communicators and people. That kind of improvement is especially important in educational organizations since communication is at the heart of everything educators do. Our schools are only as good as the conversations within them.

What Is a Better Conversation?

Many of the ideas I write about in this book started with a young boy who grew up in Jaboatão, Brazil. The boy, Paulo Freire, was a happy child despite the many difficulties he faced. Paulo lived through the aftermath of the financial crisis of 1929, the loss of his father at the age of 13, and when he returned to school after those trials, he was placed several years behind others his age. Although most of his classmates

---

[1]Desmond Tutu's comment is taken from his book *No Future Without Forgiveness* (2000).

were well fed and well dressed, Paulo came to school awkwardly out of place, a child coming from a poorer home dressed in ill-fitting clothes. Paulo eventually found himself playing soccer with many of the children from the poorest families in his village. His experience living and playing with those who were poorest marked him for life.

Freire's childhood in poverty taught him that his success at school was dramatically shaped by his living conditions.[2] As a result, he dedicated himself to improving the living and learning experiences of people who lived with less, and his primary focus was education. He went on to be a Harvard professor, an education minister in his home state, and one of the world's most influential educational theorists.

In *Pedagogy of the Oppressed* (1970), his best-known book, Freire criticized learning where the teacher's job is to "fill" students with whatever is being taught and turn students into "containers" or "receptacles" to be "filled." Freire refers to this approach as "banking education": The more completely teachers fill the receptacles, the better teachers they are, and the more meekly the receptacles permit themselves to be filled, the better students they are. Banking education is dehumanizing, Freire said, because it turns students into objects to be filled, rather than people authentically engaged in life-giving learning.

Freire's criticism of education can also be applied to forms of communication where people perceive audiences as objects to be influenced, persuaded, or worse, manipulated—not full partners in a conversation. I call this way of talking top-down communication.

There is a place for top-down conversations. If someone is going to get hit by a bus (literally or metaphorically), we probably shouldn't ask them how they feel about buses. We should tell them to get out of the way. We might need a top-down conversation to teach someone how to do a specific task like safety check an airplane, or to tell a friend or colleague that they need to change how they treat us, or to explain to a two-year-old toddler that he shouldn't put baby powder all over Daddy's mint vinyl recording of Miles Davis' *Kind of Blue*. There are probably important

> The teacher is of course an artist, but being an artist does not mean that he or she can make the profile, can shape the students. What the educator does in teaching is to make it possible for the students to become themselves.
>
> **—Myles Horton and Paulo Freire**
> (1999, p. 181)

---

[2] To see more about the relationship between Freire's work and life, see Gadotti (1994).

reasons to use top-down communication every day. Too often, though, we jump to top-down communication when a better conversation would be . . . better.

The alternative to top-down communication is a conversation where I position the person I'm speaking with as a full partner rather than an "audience"—a better conversation. Better conversations are grounded in both a set of beliefs and a collection of habits that are the embodiment of those beliefs. And better conversations can happen anywhere in a school: teacher to teacher, coach to coach, principal to teacher, teacher to student, student to student, and teacher to parent.

Beliefs and Habits

During one of my presentations on better conversations, a bright, young English teacher asked me a great question. "I think it's really important to be authentic," he said. "If I start to really listen to my friends, ask better questions, try to find common ground as you suggest, won't I be written me off as a fake? I worry that trying to learn and do all these ideas might make me inauthentic."

My quick response was that authenticity and good communication are not mutually exclusive terms, and that authenticity should never be an excuse for poor communication. But I wanted to come up with a better answer. That night I looked up *authentic* in the *Oxford English Dictionary* (2012) and found that *authentic*, according to the *OED*, refers to something that is "real, actual, genuine; original, first-hand; really proceeding from its stated source." In this sense, an authentic Picasso is a painting that was unquestionably painted by the master himself. An authentic person, then, would be someone who lives in a way that is completely consistent with who he or she is.

I tried to expand and deepen my understanding of the term *authentic* by revisiting my university philosophy classes and by going to the *Stanford Encyclopedia of Philosophy* (Zalta, 2015). I was reminded that our modern understanding of authenticity is shaped in large measure by what existentialist philosophers have written. Kierkegaard, for example, whose definition of authenticity was informed by his faith in God, described authentic people as those who find faith and then live with integrity in ways that are consistent with their faith (see *Purity of Heart Is to Will One Thing*, 1964).

Nietzsche, in contrast, whose definition of authenticity was grounded in his atheism, described authentic people as those who live lives that are not shaped by conventional norms and morality, but who live according to their own principles (see *Beyond Good and Evil*, 1966). In both of these definitions, authentic people are seen as those who know what they believe and who act consistently with those beliefs. As the *Stanford Encyclopedia of Philosophy* (Zalta, 2015) states, "To say that something is authentic is to say that it is what it professes to be."

Authenticity then involves two parts: (a) who we say we are and (b) what we do. Authenticity is definitely not just mindlessly reacting in whatever way feels good in the moment. To be an authentic communicator, we have to know what we believe and then we have to act in a way that is consistent with those beliefs. The journey toward having better conversations, therefore, is actually a journey toward authenticity. Both beliefs and actions (which I am referring to as habits) matter.

Beliefs. Understanding our beliefs and habits is not just a way of being authentic; understanding our beliefs and habits is also vitally important for improving how we communicate. Perhaps the major finding we've gathered from reviewing more than 1,000 communication reflection forms is that when people watch video recordings of their conversations, they are usually very surprised to see that how they act is quite different from how they thought they acted. We can believe we want to hear what others have to say, for example, and still talk too much.

Instructional coach Jenni Jones discovered this when she watched a video of herself leading a meeting. Jenni realized she was not communicating the respect she felt for her colleagues. On her reflection form she wrote that while her tone and questions were respectful, her "facial expressions were not respectful." Jenni wrote, "I am questioning, but my head is shaking no. Oops, more growth to make." More important, watching video gave Jenni some real insight into how she communicates when she feels stress. Jenni wrote:

> As the plant springs from, and could not be without, the seed, so every act of a man springs from the hidden seeds of thought, and could not have appeared without them.
>
> **—James Allen**
> (2006, p. 2)

When we got into a more heated part of the conversation, I started interrupting more and not validating the professionalism of my colleagues. I noticed that when I am under pressure, I take over the conversation. I need to make a conscious effort, in all forms of communication, to listen and validate my colleagues. When I watched the video I could see that my colleagues had more to say, but I talked over them. This is not the way to build trust.

Video can show us that our actions do not reflect our beliefs, but the opposite can also be true. If we do not genuinely respect our colleagues, even though we do everything the right way, our communication will often be unsuccessful. Many of us have experienced people who do all the right things, but whose actions lack authenticity. For example, we might talk with a salesperson who appears to be very interested in what we say, who listens to us carefully, but stops being a good listener when he realizes we are not going to buy what he is selling. We start to have better conversations when our beliefs and our habits are in alignment . . . when what we do is consistent with what we believe. For that reason, to start to have better conversations, we need to know what it is that we believe.

Knowing what we believe is a vital first step for change because what we see and do are both shaped by our assumptions, principles, or beliefs[3]—often in ways that we don't even notice. This idea is not new; many people have described how our conscious and unconscious beliefs affect our lives. Together, our beliefs represent a theory of how we interact with the world. In *Dialogue* (1999), William Isaac explains that our theories are always shaping what we see and do:

> When we undertake any task, like run a meeting, negotiate an agreement, discipline a child—even meditate—we operate from a set of taken-for-granted rules or ideas of how to be effective. Understanding these tacit rules is what I mean by *theory*. The word *theory* comes from the same roots as the word *theater*, which means simply "to see." A theory is a way of seeing . . . Without a theory, however—some way to

---

[3] I use the words *beliefs* and *assumptions* interchangeably.

assess what is happening—we shall be forever doomed to operate blindly, subject to chance. (p. 73, italics in original)

Our beliefs give shape to who we are and what we do. We can hold them as individuals, or we can hold them collectively as part of the culture of an organization. In *Organizational Culture and Leadership* (2010), Edgar Schein writes that culture at its deepest level is also a set of beliefs:

Culture as a set of basic assumptions defines for us what to pay attention to, what things mean, how to react emotionally to what is going on, and what actions to take in various kinds of situations. After we have developed an integrated set of such assumptions—a "thought world" or "mental map"—we will be maximally comfortable with others who share the same set of assumptions and very uncomfortable and vulnerable in situations where different assumptions operate because either we will not understand what is going on, or worse, we will misperceive and misinterpret the actions of others. (p. 29)

In a number of other publications, I have written about partnership principles (see, for example, *Unmistakable Impact: A Partnership Approach for Dramatically Improving Instruction*, 2011). At its core, partnership is about a simple idea—to treat others the way we want to be treated—and partnership stands at the heart of better conversations. When we see the people with whom we interact as partners, there are certain Better Conversations Beliefs we usually adopt. Those beliefs, explained in detail in Chapter 2, are the following:

1. I see conversation partners as equals.

2. I want to hear what others have to say.

3. I believe people should have a lot of autonomy.

4. I don't judge others.

5. Conversation should be back and forth.

6. Conversation should be life-giving.

Habits. I have chosen to describe the practices in this book as habits rather than strategies, tactics, or some other word that describes what we do. Of course, within habits there are strategies. The habit of building emotional connection, for example, involves the strategy of being mindful of others' bids for connection. I've chosen *habits* as my key term because I think the best way to imagine communication practices is as a collection of *habits*. Indeed, this book is really about helping us become aware of our ineffective communication habits so we can replace them with effective habits.

Many have written about habits. I first started thinking about habitual practice when I read Stephen Covey's classic book *The 7 Habits of Highly Effective People* (1987). Covey explained that habits have a powerful hold over our behavior, and developing the right habits was critical to becoming an effective person. Comparing the struggle to break a habit to the force it takes for a rocket to pull away from the Earth's gravitational force, Covey wrote:

> Breaking deeply imbedded habitual tendencies such as procrastination, impatience, criticalness, or selfishness that violate basic principles of human effectiveness involves more than just a little willpower and a few minor changes in our lives. "Lift off" takes a tremendous effort, but once we break out of the gravity pull, our freedom takes on a whole new dimension. (p. 47)

More recently, journalist Charles Duhigg, in *The Power of Habit: Why We Do What We Do in Life and Business* (2012), summarizes much of the research on habits. Duhigg provides some useful definitions. A habit, he says, "is a formula our brain automatically follows" (p. 285); "a choice that we deliberately make at some point, and then stop thinking about, but continue doing, often every day" (p. 284). My hope is that this book will give people the tools so that they learn and practice the Better Conversations Habits until they become "a formula our brain automatically follows."

Habits can be good or bad. Habits of asking good questions, sharing positive information, or not interrupting can all lead to better conversations. But habits of talking too much, taking too much credit, or jumping to negative assumptions can be damaging. In *What Got You Here Won't Get You There: How Successful People Get Even More Successful* (2007), Marshall Goldsmith writes specifically about habits and communication:

> We are what we repeatedly do. Excellence, then, is not an act, but a habit.
>
> **—Aristotle**

> [the communication problems people have] . . . are not deep-seated neuroses that require years of therapy or tons of medication to erase. More often than not, they are simply behavioral ticks—bad habits that we repeat dozens of times a day in the workplace—which can be cured by (a) pointing them out, (b) showing the havoc they cause among the people surrounding us, and (c) demonstrating that with a slight behavioral tick we can achieve a much more appealing effect. (p. 9)

Learning to Have Better Conversations

This book will only help people have better conversations if they adopt some or all of the Better Conversations Beliefs and Habits for themselves. For that reason, I describe different approaches people can take to learn and internalize the Beliefs and Habits. People can learn the Better Conversations Beliefs and Habits on their own, with a partner, a coach, a team, or an entire school or district.

Changing our beliefs and habits involves two kinds of knowledge: explicit and tacit. Explicit knowledge is knowledge we can describe, discuss, and easily share—the knowledge described in checklists, manuals, how-to guides, and books like this one. Tacit knowledge, in contrast, is knowledge we have but that we don't know we have. As Michael Polanyi (1958), who first described tacit knowledge, has written, "we can know more than we can tell" (p. 60).

Nonaka and Takeuchi's classic study of learning in organizations, *The Knowledge Creating Company: How Japanese Companies Create the Dynamics of Innovation* (1995), describes the roles explicit and tacit knowledge play in innovation and knowledge sharing. Explicit knowledge, they write, "can be transmitted across individuals formally and easily [since it] can be articulated in formal language including grammatical statements, mathematical expressions, speci-fications, manuals, and so forth" (p. viii). Tacit knowledge, the researchers write, "is a more important kind of knowl-edge" (p. viii). Tacit knowledge "is personal knowledge embedded in individual experience and involves intangi-ble factors such as personal belief, perspective, and the value systems" (p. viii).

According to Nonaka and Takeuchi, as depicted in the figure below, organizational learning involves three stages: (a) becoming aware of our tacit current beliefs and habits (tacit knowledge), (b) taking in descriptions of better ways of communicating (explicit knowledge), and then (c) prac-ticing those ideas until they become new beliefs and habits (tacit again).

This book gives you the tools you need to move from tacit to explicit to tacit knowledge. It also includes the com-ments of others who also employed this methodology to improve their communication skills. Ben Collins, for exam-ple, an assistant principal from Des Plaines, Illinois, told me that self-coaching himself on the habit of making emotional connections was vitally important for his personal and pro-fessional growth. "I have learned to be a kinder, more atten-tive person through the process," Ben told me, "and it never would have happened if I hadn't coached myself."

Ben began by video recording himself in conversation. He learned that he was missing many opportunities to con-nect with other people. "Before self-coaching," Ben wrote in his coaching log,

> I wouldn't have thought as much about connecting with other people. Now I'm better at capitalizing on opportunities to connect. Too often in the past I used to let moments pass and that has probably affected my relationships even more than I know. Today I have a type of radar out for those times where I can

share a connection with someone, and that has made me much more present in my professional and personal life.

Ben moved from not knowing his habits or tacit knowledge, to learning the new habit of emotional connection explicitly described in this book, to practicing those explicit practices until they became almost habitual for him. As Ben told me in a conversation, "These ideas have helped me be a better professional and helped me be better with my fiancé. But that only happened because I took the time to coach myself."

The process Ben employed can be employed by anyone. At the end of each chapter are three different kinds of reflection forms people can use to learn and adopt the Better Conversations Beliefs and Habits. *Looking Back* forms can be used to analyze conversations to identify effective and ineffective habits and beliefs that are already in place. *Looking At* forms can be used to clarify and deepen knowledge of new habits. *Looking Ahead* forms can be used to plan implementation of new habits.

An essential part of learning these beliefs and habits involves using a smartphone or tablet to video record your conversations. If we are going to try to get better, we need to understand our current reality (our beliefs and habits). The easiest way to get a clear picture of reality when it comes to understanding how we communicate is by recording ourselves talking.

Thanks to technological advances, today there is simply no real reason not to try to get better. Never before has it been so easy for us to coach ourselves on our communication skills. Anyone with a smartphone or tablet can push the red button, record a conversation (when their conversation partner is agreeable), and see how effectively they listen, build emotional connections, foster dialogue, and so forth. The little computer in our pocket helps us clearly see our current reality, set goals, and monitor our progress toward those goals. With a little effort, we can quickly, permanently, and dramatically improve our relationships with others.

It may seem a bit weird to sit down with your six-year-old daughter or a teacher you are coaching and record your conversation on your iPhone. Indeed, you might be tempted

I think you are in the worst position possible to make any judgments about yourself until you see yourself from the different perspective video offers. Video helped me be more aware of myself and others and how we connect. I started to notice that there are times that certain people had kind of a default condition that they would use when they related to others. I started to think to myself, "I wonder if that's me?" I started to really pay attention to other people and acknowledge them when they were speaking and to make sure that I smiled more. I started noticing that people who smile—I just want to be around them more frequently. I noticed that my body language changed a little bit, too. I am an administrator, and we have had some pretty intense conversations. Just trying to be a good person goes a long way when you are trying to make emotional connections with people.

—Ben Collins,
Assistant Principal,
Des Plaines, Illinois

to skip video recording since it is so out of the ordinary pattern of our lives. However, if much of our effectiveness and happiness truly depends on effective communication, then perhaps we need to get over our awkwardness of being video recorded and just do it.

You can start by video recording one conversation. Just seeing yourself in conversation can be a huge catalyst for change. After recording the conversation, you should review it by completing the *Looking Back* form. After that, you can deepen your knowledge of the habit you're studying by reading an appropriate chapter in the book and using the *Looking At* form. Then you can plan to implement a new habit using the *Looking Ahead* form. Finally, you can continue to practice implementing the habit by video recording new conversations and using the *Looking Back* form to monitor progress. If you use video and this book to improve your communication habits, you will improve the way you interact with others, and that will improve your life.

The Better Conversations Beliefs and Habits can be implemented in many different ways. The most common processes are as follows.

On Your Own. Most of the people who learned and practiced the ideas in this book did so on their own. To do this, they recorded conversations, used the *Looking Back* forms to analyze their conversations, and then used the *Looking At* and *Looking Ahead* forms to implement the ideas.

With a Partner. Two or more colleagues can collaborate to improve their communication skills. For example, they might simply meet to discuss what they are discovering as they are learning on their own, or they might share their forms as they complete them. Perhaps the most powerful way to learn is for partners to share with each other their videos and completed forms, discuss what they learned from each video and form, and then problem solve together how they might both improve.

With a Coach. People can also improve their communication skills by working with an instructional coach. In such a scenario, the coach would have a deep knowledge of the

Video forced me to take a hard look at my coaching skills and practices, as well as my relationships with the staff I work with. I have realized the true power of video through watching myself interact with others, and it has made me more willing and excited to continue using video to improve my communication skills. I genuinely want to hear what the teacher is saying so that we can focus our efforts on improving student learning. If I improve, I can be more effective, and self-awareness is a big key to making any ongoing change. Video and self-reflection made me aware of some habits that I want to change, but never would have realized without video.

—**Shana Olson,**
Instructional Coach, Hillside Elementary, West Des Moines, Iowa

Better Conversations Beliefs and Habits. Coaches would partner with others by reviewing videos, asking questions to identify goals, explaining habits precisely, modeling habits, helping others implement the new habits, and monitor progress until goals are met.

With a Team. Much can be learned by collaborating with a team. Most often, each time the team meets, one team member shares video and hosts a discussion about what worked, what didn't work, and what might be done differently in the future. Team members might also complete and share their *Looking Back, Looking At,* and *Looking Ahead* forms.

Across an Organization. Whole schools or districts can collaborate to learn the Better Conversations Beliefs and Habits. This might start with a workshop from consultants at the Instructional Coaching Group (instructionalcoaching.com) or in some other way. Once people have been introduced to the Better Conversations Beliefs and Habits, they can move forward using one of the ways mentioned above—learning on their own, with partners, coaches, or teams.

What You Will Find in This Book

Chapter 2: The Better Conversations Beliefs. What we do is the result of how we *think and act,* and learning how to have better conversations starts with beliefs. This chapter provides an overview of the six beliefs that are at the heart of better conversations and explains simple things people can do to surface and clarify what their beliefs are and what they would like them to be.

Chapter 3: Listening With Empathy. The most important communication habit is listening. When someone listens to us attentively, we feel respected. Habit 1, Demonstrating Empathy, is a necessary first step for listening. Habit 2, Listening With Empathy, puts the habit of empathy into practice. We can listen effectively by (a) committing to listening, (b) focusing on others rather than ourselves, (c) pausing to ensure we open up conversations rather than shut them down, and (d) not interrupting.

Chapter 4: Fostering Dialogue. When two or more people communicate in a way that makes it possible for them to "think together," they move toward Habit 3, Fostering Dialogue. This involves balancing advocacy and inquiry, sharing our ideas, and encouraging others' ideas and questions.

Chapter 5: Asking Better Questions. We can improve our questions by asking open (opinion) questions and by being nonjudgmental. Better questions create conversations that pique curiosity, foster engagement, and keep us fully present.

Chapter 6: Connecting. John Gottman is one of the world's leading experts on relationships, and he identifies emotional connection as the critical variable that leads to healthy versus unhealthy conversations. Gottman sees emotional connection manifested in bids for connection and responses to those bids, which he refers to as turning toward, turning away, and turning against. Habit 5, Making Emotional Connections, involves learning how to make and respond to bids that positively affect how connected we feel toward others and how connected they feel toward us.

One powerful way to connect is to share positive information with others. Most of us, however, probably share positive information in a way that isn't effective. Habit 6, Being a Witness to the Good, involves effectively sharing positive information by sharing comments that are specific, direct, and nonattributive.

Chapter 7: Finding Common Ground. Since we are frequently reminded of the ways in which we are different from each other, we can be overly obsessed with our dissimilarities. Habit 7, Finding Common Ground, involves a better approach, turning away from our obvious differences and building our relationships on what we hold in common. We can do that by considering how our Interests, Convictions, Activities, Roles, and Experiences (I-CARE) can divide us or provide a way to find what we hold in common with others.

Chapter 8: Redirecting Toxic Words and Emotions. The lifeblood of the culture of any school or organization is the way people talk, so part of strong leadership is shaping the organizational culture one conversation at a time. On occasion, this may require redirecting conversations that are not good for the school or the people in the school. We must also pay attention to the toxic emotions that exist within us. No matter what your beliefs and habits, if you do not control your emotions, they will dramatically interfere with your ability to have better conversations. Habit 8, Controlling Toxic Emotions, involves a simple set of strategies we can use to (a) identify when our emotions come into play, (b) uncover the cause of our emotional response, (c) identify what we can do to reframe a potentially volatile conversation, and (d) determine how to maintain control even when we might have ample reason to react emotionally. Habit 9, Redirecting Toxic Conversations, involves recognizing the kinds of conversations that are unacceptable, and identifying strategies people can use to redirect those conversations.

Chapter 9: Building Trust. Trust is a critical factor for meaningful conversation. When we don't trust someone, we hesitate to be open, vulnerable, or candid. Habit 10, Building Trust, involves increasing trust by increasing our credibility, competence, and warmth, and by maintaining a focus on others rather than ourselves.

Each chapter begins with a learning map that displays the key ideas in the chapter and some of the ways in which those ideas are connected. Each chapter concludes with a To Sum Up section that restates some of the most important ideas in the chapter and a Going Deeper section that includes suggested books you can read to learn more about each new habit.

At the end of Chapters 3–9 are *Looking Back, Looking At,* or *Looking Ahead* forms. The forms provide a way to look back on interactions and reflect on what was learned, a way to look at a habit to deepen understanding, and a way to look ahead to prepare to implement the Better Conversations Habits.

> **The Better Conversations Habits**
>
> 1. Demonstrating Empathy
> 2. Listening With Empathy
> 3. Fostering Dialogue
> 4. Asking Better Questions
> 5. Making Emotional Connections
> 6. Being a Witness to the Good
> 7. Finding Common Ground
> 8. Controlling Toxic Emotions
> 9. Redirecting Toxic Conversations
> 10. Building Trust

TO SUM UP

Better conversations involve beliefs and habits. The six beliefs that stand at the heart of better conversations are the following: (1) I see conversation partners as equals,

(2) I want to hear what others have to say, (3) I believe people should have a lot of autonomy, (4) I don't judge others, (5) conversation should be back and forth, and (6) conversation should be life-giving.

The ten Better Conversations Habits are the following: (1) demonstrating empathy, (2) listening with empathy, (3) fostering dialogue, (4) asking better questions, (5) making emotional connections, (6) being a witness to the good, (7) finding common ground, (8) controlling toxic emotions, (9) redirecting toxic conversations, and (10) building trust.

To internalize the Better Conversations Beliefs and Habits, we need to become aware of what Michael Polanyi refers to as tacit knowledge (the beliefs and habits we embrace without even knowing it), learn explicit knowledge (the beliefs and habits described in this book), and then practice them until they become tacit (habits we use all the time when we are engaged in conversations).

We can learn the Better Conversations Beliefs and Habits on our own, with a partner, coach, team, or even with all the employees in a school or district.

GOING DEEPER

There are a few foundational books that have profoundly shaped my overall understanding of how we should interact with others. I read Paulo Freire's *Pedagogy of the Oppressed* (1970) when I was a 20-year-old fairly apathetic university student. Few readings made an impact on me when I first tried out postsecondary education, but Freire's book totally caught my imagination, and it continues to do so today. Freire gave me words to describe what I felt was true about learning and human interaction. He also taught me that when we engage in conversations in which everyone feels safe to share ideas and think together, we help people become better. Freire showed me that the opposite is also true: We dehumanize people when we don't give them an opportunity to say what they think.

Peter Block's *Stewardship: Choosing Service Over Self-Interest* (1993) truly changed my worldview by introducing me to the idea that we should position ourselves as partners when we interact with others. Partnership has become one of the most important concepts in my work and life, and it plays a big role in the book you are reading. Although *Stewardship* is a business book, I find Block's ideas about power in organizations to be very relevant to schools and classrooms.

Margaret Wheatley's *Turning to One Another: Simple Conversations to Restore Hope to the Future* (2002), more than any other book, communicated to me the potential of respectful conversation. Wheatley's book is a beautiful, inspiring testament to the power, as the subtitle says, of simple conversations. *Turning to One Another* is not a book of strategies, but more a work of art proclaiming just how important it is for us to treat each other as fully human.

Better Conversations Beliefs

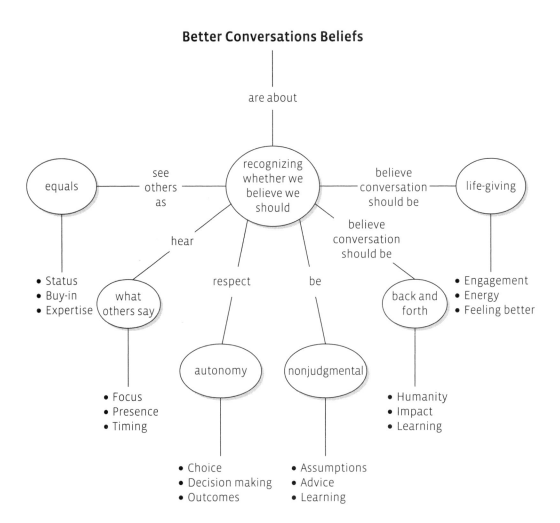

THE BETTER
CONVERSATIONS BELIEFS

*A dialogue or conversation among individuals . . . must
be based on mutual respect, equality, a willingness to
listen and to risk one's prejudices and opinions.*

—Bernstein (1983, pp. 219–220)

*It is amazing how often we move to positions of power
when we are not consciously aware of the need to stay
in good communication with others.*

—Marilyn Allen, Coordinator of
Student Services, Saskatoon, Saskatchewan

Jane is an assistant principal in a small rural school
district in Northern Alberta, Canada. Before she became
an administrator, Jane wanted to learn about instructional
coaching, and after searching online, she discovered the
coaching conferences we offer in Lawrence, Kansas. She
couldn't afford to pay for the traveling costs to come to
Kansas, and her district couldn't afford to send her, so Jane
looked for other ways to get funding. After doing some
research, she discovered a grant that would fund her trip if
she could demonstrate that she was an outstanding teacher.
Jane wrote a proposal and won the funds.

In October 2011, Jane came to Kansas and attended every workshop we offered. She spent two and a half weeks learning about coaching, video and learning, high-impact instruction, and coaching coaches. She ended her visit by attending our annual Teaching, Learning, and Coaching conference. Jane was a model participant, bright, enthusiastic, and constantly trying to learn as much as she could. I expected Jane to be tired out after all the sessions she attended, six days a week for two and half weeks. But she left on the last day of our conference more enthusiastic than ever. She couldn't wait to go back to her school and put what she had learned into practice.

Jane stayed in contact after she returned home, and she asked me to Skype into her school to talk about instruction. Ordinarily I would resist doing this because I hate sitting in a room listening to somebody talk on Skype, and I assume others feel the same. However, I couldn't resist Jane's persistent request. She was a determined, optimistic educational leader, and soon she was promoted to assistant principal.

Unfortunately, the principal of Jane's school was not as motivated a leader as Jane. He and I met at a conference I gave in Canada, when Jane brought him with her, and he was a friendly, easy-going man. However, he soon made it clear he hadn't signed up to be an instructional leader and would be retiring soon. He was willing to let Jane do her "coaching thing," but his goal was to get through his last 19 months with as little stress as possible. Jane told me the school's staff was at sea over the lack of leadership, and consequently, any growth that occurred happened sporadically. There was no coherence, no vision, no follow-through, and sadly, no growth.

In the summer after her principal retired and before a new principal was put in place, a district supervisor asked Jane to meet with him for a conversation. This is the conversation Jane described when she practiced Habit 8, Controlling Toxic Emotions, as part of our global communication study. On her reflection form, Jane described the conversation:

> I believed that I was "invited" to have a learning conversation to assist me to apply for principal positions, but I discovered the supervisor had a different agenda. His purpose for inviting me was to

place blame for my school's standardized test scores directly on my shoulders. For 90 minutes he challenged my competence, professionalism, and ethics—and mostly he just treated me with disdain.

The supervisor didn't know about the lack of leadership in the school, and he apparently didn't want to hear about it. Jane tried to remain in control while she was berated, but as she wrote on her reflection form, "My surprise and anger gave way to tears of frustration and disbelief." More than a year after that conversation, Jane recently told me, she still vividly remembers that day.

Jane is a highly motivated, smart, and emotionally intelligent professional. She is exactly the kind of person her school needs. She has stayed where she is because she cares about the students and the staff, but the conversation she experienced made it difficult for her to feel enthusiastic about her work.

When I saw Jane recently at another conference in Canada, she was clearly frustrated and disappointed by the lack of support she felt. Jane worked overtime to move her school forward, but the supervisor's tongue-lashing had clearly depleted some of her energy. How could the supervisor treat such a bright professional so poorly? How could anyone think that such a damaging conversation would actually make things better?

There are at least two reasons people act the way Jane's supervisor acted: Either they are unaware of their behavior (and there is plenty of evidence from our study that people are often unaware of how they act during conversations), or they consciously or unconsciously work from a set of beliefs that lead them to act in such dehumanizing ways. Often, people act without even pausing to consider what they believe about how they interact with others. Unfortunately, when people don't think carefully about their beliefs, they can find themselves engaging in far too many unsuccessful conversations.

Jane's memory of her time with her supervisor, like anyone's memories of a conversation, could be colored by any number of perceptual errors. I wasn't there, and I can't assess the accuracy of her description. Nevertheless, two things hold true. First, the conversation did not motivate Jane and therefore did not benefit the children in Jane's

> I've learned a lot by reading through the materials, practicing the activities, and changing entrenched responses. I have slowed down, learned to listen, and become keenly aware of choices I have in communicating with those I come in contact. This has become a very empowering series of skills.
>
> —**Research volunteer**

school. Second, it is not uncommon for people to experience conversations where they feel the way Jane felt when she talked with her supervisor.[1]

We do not need to experience so many destructive conversations. One encouraging finding in our global communication study is that most people were able to learn new habits that improved their conversations. Instructional coach Deb Bidulka, for example, wrote, "I believe I am on my way to being a better communicator. I am entering conversations in my personal and work life conscious of the strategies, and I am being more authentic in all conversations."

One way to improve conversations is to identify what we really want to believe about how we interact with others. We are not slaves to our beliefs. We get to choose them, but to do so, we must surface our current beliefs and then consider what alternative beliefs might better describe who we are and who we want to be. Each of the Better Conversations Beliefs is described below so that you can consider what you believe today and what you would like to believe in the future.

The Better Conversations Beliefs

1. I see conversation partners as equals.

2. I want to hear what others have to say.

3. I believe people should have a lot of autonomy.

4. I don't judge others.

5. Conversation should be back and forth.

6. Conversation should be life-giving.

Belief 1: I See Conversation Partners as Equals

The conversation Jane experienced with her supervisor is an extreme example. More frequently, the inequality inherent in top-down conversations is more subtly expressed. A young principal deeply committed to the children in her school and keen to lead the school in the right direction might find herself in top-down conversations because she thinks that is the way she is supposed to interact. For example, she might observe a lesson, identify what she thought went well, identify three things the teacher should work on, and then try to convince the teacher to "buy in" to her suggestions. To her, that seems like what a principal should do. Unfortunately, that kind of top-down conversation is often unsuccessful.

---

[1]A 2007 Zogby survey of U.S. adults found that 37% of the nearly 8,000 respondents experienced bullying conversations similar to the one Jane experienced (results are reported in Sutton, 2010, p. 4).

Miller and Rollnick identify six kinds of "advocacy responses" (what I call top-down approaches to communication) that can engender resistance.

1. **Arguing for Change.** The counselor directly takes up the pro-change side of ambivalence on a particular issue and seeks to persuade the client to make the change.

2. **Assuming the Expert Role.** The counselor structures the conversation in a way that communicates the counselor "has the answers." This includes the question–answer trap of asking many closed-ended questions as well as lecturing the client.

3. **Criticizing, Shaming, or Blaming.** The counselor's underlying intent seems to be to shock or jar the client into changing by instilling negative emotions about the status quo (p. 50).

4. **Labeling.** The counselor proposes acceptance of a specific label or diagnosis to characterize or explain the client's behavior. The focus is on what the client "is" or "has" rather than on what he or she does (p. 50).

5. **Being in a Hurry.** Sometimes a perceived shortness of time causes the counselor to believe that clear, forceful tactics are called for in order to get through. From his experience in working with horses, Monty Roberts (1997) has observed the paradox that "if you act like you only have a few minutes" it can take all day to accomplish a change, whereas "if you act like you have all day," it may take only a few minutes. In counseling, this most often takes the form of getting ahead of your client's readiness.

6. **Claiming Preeminence.** Finally, resistance is invoked when a counselor claims preeminence—that the counselor's goals and perspectives override those of the client. The quintessential form is a paternalistic "I-know-what-is-best-for-you" approach (p. 50).

In *Helping: How to Offer, Give, and Receive Help* (2009), Edgar Schein, an MIT researcher most famous for his seminal work studying culture, explains that when people position themselves as superior, as the principal above has inadvertently done, they create an unequal relationship that inhibits communication and professional learning. According to Schein, people only feel conversations have been successful when they are given the status they think they deserve:

When a conversation has not been equitable we sometimes feel offended. That usually means that the value we have claimed for ourselves has not been acknowledged, or that the other person or persons did not realize who we were or how important our communication was. (p. 30)

The new principal had good intentions, and she likely cares deeply about her staff, but there is a good chance her approach would engender resistance. She might find that when she tells teachers what they should do, they "resist" and explain why her ideas won't work or that they've already tried those ideas and they didn't succeed.

The reason people resist ideas in top-down conversations often has nothing to do with the ideas: It has to do with their perception that they are not getting the status they deserve. Miller and Rollnick, who have spent decades studying therapeutic relationships, have found that the way a therapist approaches a client can become a major barrier to change. In their classic work, *Motivational Interviewing: Preparing People for Change* (2002), the authors write that

the way in which one communicates can make it more or less likely that a person will change ... Counsel in a direct, confrontational manner, and client resistance goes up. Counsel in a reflective, supportive manner, and resistance goes down while change increases. (pp. 8–9)

Most people living in democracies, without giving the idea much thought, would quickly say that they believe all people are equal. Democratic political systems are founded on the basic belief that everyone deserves to be treated equally. In most democratic countries, equality means that everyone should have equal access to schools, the opportunity to vote, certain human rights, and so forth. In a democracy, I also have the equal opportunity to pursue my own personal and career goals and make my own mistakes. At its core, to believe everyone is equal is to believe everyone counts the same.

People say they believe that everyone is equal, but often, especially when they find themselves in positions of power, their actions show otherwise. Robert Sutton, in *Good Boss, Bad Boss: How to Be the Best . . . and Learn from the Worst* (2010), summarizes many studies Dacher Keltner conducted looking at the influence of power. Keltner's studies are damning. He reports,

> When researchers give people power in scientific experiments, they are more likely to touch others in potentially inappropriate ways, to flirt in a more direct fashion, to interrupt others, to speak out of turn, to fail to look at others when they are speaking, and to tease friends and colleagues in hostile and humiliating fashion. (pp. 220–221)

"There is strong evidence," Sutton writes, summarizing Keltner's research, "that power turns people into insensitive jerks who are oblivious to subordinates' needs and actions" (p. 221).

An alternative to the top-down conversation is a conversation grounded in equality. When I believe others are equal to me, I should never see myself as superior to them. In a better conversation, I intentionally look to see my conversation partner's strengths—and I communicate in some way that I know them.

I have watched many hours of video of instructional coaches interacting with teachers. The coaches who believe in equality constantly communicate that they see their collaborating teachers as equals. Coaches who embrace equality position their collaborating teachers as decision makers. They sit beside rather than across from their teachers, make eye contact, listen, and draw out their collaborating teachers' expertise.

Ric Palma was an instructional coach for many years in Topeka, Kansas, and in an interview for my book *Instructional Coaching* (2007), Ric told me that he wants people to walk away from conversations feeling valued. "I let them know that their opinions matter," Ric told me, "and I draw on their knowledge and expertise. They see me as someone who is coming in as one of them, instead of somebody who is coming in to impart all this knowledge."

Lynn Barnes Schuster, an instructional coach in the Katy, Texas School District, told me when I was writing *Unmistakable Impact* (2011) that she takes a "servitude attitude." We have to "care about the people we are serving," Lynn told me. "We can't go in like the know-it-all expert. Coaches have to find a way to harness the hope and make it work for both teachers and students."

Belief 2: I Want to Hear What Others Have to Say

Deb Bidulka is a learning support facilitator for Prairie Spirit School Division in Saskatoon, Saskatchewan, Canada. For our global communication study, when Deb experimented with Habit 2, Listening With Empathy, she found herself teaching a high school class that included a student whom she had been warned had a "hot temper." On her reflection form, Deb tells her story as follows:

> Student voice is when a student expresses an opinion, it is heard by the teacher, and something is done.
>
> **—Sixth-grade male student,** quoted in Quaglia & Corso (2014, p. 1)

I had been forewarned this student had a hot temper, and he did. He disrupted the class I was teaching. To try and get to the root of his issues, I asked the student to come and talk with me at the end of class. I anticipated that he would be defensive and angry, and might want to lash out. I was angry too, but I knew if I let anger rule the conversation the problem would escalate.

I started out the conversation by telling the student I wanted to know what needed to happen so he could experience success in the class. This worked well as the student was taken aback. I focused on solution finding rather than blaming the student or focusing on what he was doing wrong. He ended up sharing critical personal information that helped us come up with a solution together. He ended up being very successful in my class.

Deb's experiences illustrate a finding that is reinforced by Russell J. Quaglia and Michael J. Corso's findings reported in *Student Voice: The Instrument of Change* (2014)—student voice matters a great deal. Quaglia and Corso write:

student voice is not yet a reality in most classrooms and schools. The national My Voice survey, administered to 56,877 students in Grades 6–12 in the

2012–13 school year by the Pearson Foundation, reports that just 46% feel students have a voice in decision making at their school and just 52% believe that teachers are willing to learn from students (Quaglia Institute for Student Aspirations [QISA], 2013) . . . less than half [of the surveyed students] (45%) say they are valued members of their school community. (p. 2)

What Quaglia and Corso (2014) found with respect to students is also true for adults—they want to be heard, and too often they are not, especially, as it turns out, if they are teachers. Marcus Buckingham and Curt Coffman reviewed surveys of over a million employees and 90-minute interviews of over 80,000 managers to identify characteristics of a strong workplace. In *First Break All the Rules: What the World's Greatest Managers Do Differently* (1999), the researchers synthesized their findings into 12 questions, with the idea that employees who answer yes to all 12 questions are more likely to be engaged and motivated. The seventh question on the list was, "At work, do my opinions seem to count?" Employees who are engaged by their work report that they believe that what they have to say is important to their organizations.

Researcher Shane Lopez, the author of *Making Hope Happen: Create the Future You Want for Yourself and Others* (2013), works with the Gallup Organization where Buckingham and Coffman worked when their book was written. Shane also lives in my hometown, Lawrence, Kansas, and we met for lunch two years ago to discuss a keynote presentation Shane was going to give at our Teaching, Learning, and Coaching conference.

Sitting in 715 Mass—a noisy, bustling restaurant in downtown Lawrence—I asked Shane about his most recent research. Shane told me that he was about to release a study he had done with Pretty Sidhu that looked at which categories of employees answered yes to the question, "At work, do my opinions seem to count?"

Shane leaned in to tell me the results. "We looked at over 150,000 surveys. We looked at a wide range of employees, managers, physicians, nurses, K–12 teachers, construction workers, service workers, and more. Guess who came in last on the list? Teachers. Teachers felt their opinions counted

> What people really need is a good listening to.
>
> **—Marylou Casey,** quoted in Miller & Rollnick (2002, p. 52)

less than construction workers and service workers. Teachers were at the bottom of the list."[2]

Lopez's finding suggests that it is especially important we listen to educators since so many report their opinions are not heard. Stephen Covey's (1989) phrase "seek first to understand, then be understood" describes a simple way we can encourage people to do just that. We can enter into conversations by asking questions and making sure we understand what others are saying before we give our opinions. By temporarily setting aside our own opinions, we can really hear what others have to say and powerfully demonstrate that we respect others' perspectives. When we listen with empathy to others' ideas, thoughts, and concerns, we communicate that others' lives are important and meaningful.

When I want to hear what others have to say, I should be fully present in conversations. I may be someone's boss or teacher, but I shouldn't confuse structural power with real power. Indeed, if I think I am a better, more valuable, more worthy person than others, I won't be engaging in a better conversation.

Belief 3: People Should Have a Lot of Autonomy

Recently, I had a meeting with a group of instructional coaches and administrators from a large district in the United States. The people at the meeting talked about the excitement they felt about coaching's potential to make a difference in children's lives and shared their hopes and fears as they looked forward to a new school year. One experienced coach spoke for the group when she talked about her most pressing concerns.

"Our principal has already told the staff our three priorities for next year," she said. "And already we're getting pushback (from the teachers). I'm not sure how to coach them if they refuse to do what they are told."

The truth is, of course, that the teachers in the school are just like everyone else—none of us likes to be told what to

---

[2]When this book was written, these results were available online at http://www.gallup.com/poll/163745/newer-teachers-likely-engaged-work.aspx.

do. Edward Deci and Richard Ryan have dedicated their lives to studying motivation, and one of their major findings is that people are rarely motivated by other people's plans for them. As Deci writes in *Why We Do What We Do: Understanding Self-Motivation* (1995),

> control is an easy answer. It . . . sounds tough, so it feels reassuring to people who believe things have gone awry . . . however, it has become increasingly clear that the approach simply does not work . . . the widespread reliance on rewards and punishments to motivate responsibility has failed to yield the desired results. Indeed, mounting evidence suggests that these so-called solutions, based on the principle of rigid authority, are exacerbating rather than ameliorating the problems. (pp. 1–2)

Leaders may feel a reassuring sense of control when they come up with a plan, explain it, and expect others to comply and implement it. However, a plan means little if it isn't implemented, and when professionals have no voice in a plan and are told what to do, they are unlikely to be motivated to embrace the plan. Top-down directives might create the illusion of a solution, but Deci and Ryan's work suggests such directives will only, at best, lead to half-hearted compliance and won't inspire the kind of commitment needed for real, meaningful change.

An alternative to the top-down model is to start by recognizing that people, especially professionals, need to have some autonomy to be motivated. Deci writes that "to be autonomous"

> means to act in accord with one's self—it means feeling free and volitional in one's actions. When autonomous, people are fully willing to do what they are doing, and they embrace the activity with a sense of interest and commitment. Their actions emanate from their true sense of self, so they are being authentic. In contrast, to be controlled means to act because one is pressured. When controlled, people act without a sense of personal endorsement. Their behavior is not an expression of the self, for the self has been subjugated to the controls. (p. 2)

When you're in a conversation, your brain has to do three things at once: Stay in the content of the conversation, read the person or people you are talking with, and read yourself. It's that last part that really separates the successful people in education.

—**Ben Collins,**
Assistant Principal,
Des Plaines, Illinois

Respecting others' needs for autonomy is both a practical and a good thing to do. It is practical because people will not be motivated to change or embrace what we have to say unless they have real choices. The surest way to ensure that someone doesn't do something, whether they are 6 or 66 years old, is to tell them they have to do it. In Timothy Gallwey's words (2001), "When you insist, they will resist."

Respecting others' needs for autonomy is also a good thing to do simply because trying to control others is dehumanizing. As Freire (1970) says, "freedom . . . is the indispensable condition for the quest for human completion . . . without freedom [we] cannot exist authentically" (p. 31). Similarly, Peter Block (1993) emphasizes the primacy of choice: "Saying no is the fundamental way we have of differentiating ourselves. To take away my right to say no is to claim sovereignty over me . . . If we cannot say no, then saying yes has no meaning" (pp. 30–31). When we see those we communicate with as equal partners, we inevitably see them as autonomous people who should make their own choices. Partners don't tell their partners what to do.

When we recognize other people's need for autonomy, it changes the way we communicate. Since we recognize that others will make their own decisions about what we share, we offer ideas provisionally, leaving room for our partners to come to their own conclusions, rather than choosing to simply tell others what to do.

Autonomy is as important for young people as it is for adults. As Jim Fay and David Funk have written in *Teaching With Love and Logic: Taking Control of the Classroom* (1995), "We all want to have some control over our lives and when we feel we are losing that control we will fight to the end to get it back" (p. 69). Recognizing the importance of control, Fay and Funk identify shared control as one of the four key principles of their love and logic approach. They write, "when we allow kids to have some control over their own learning, they often amaze even the most experienced teacher" (p. 212).

> Wise teachers know the more small choices they provide, the fewer big problems they have.
>
> **—Jim Fay and Charles Fay**
> (2001)

Belief 4: I Don't Judge Others

My mentor, dissertation advisor, and lifelong friend Don Deshler perfectly embodies equality in the way he interacts with people. If anyone has a right to feel a bit superior, it should be Don. He has a résumé with more than 35 pages of publications, was chosen by the president to sit on the Presidential Advisory Committee on Literacy, and was chosen by the Council for Exceptional Children as one of the ten most influential people in special education in the 20th century.

By any standard, Don is an incredibly successful and powerful professional. However, the reality is that whenever I talk with Don, and I have talked with him hundreds of times over the past two decades, he makes me feel like I am doing him a favor to have the conversation. Don listens, encourages, and asks great questions. What characterizes each of my conversations with Don is that I feel safe to say whatever is on my mind. Don never makes me feel like he is negatively judging me. In fact, I feel just the opposite—more than anything else, I feel Don communicates that he sees me as a valuable person.

Don's nonjudgmental way of interacting informs the way he communicates in all settings. When he leads a meeting, gives a presentation, has a conversation about a university employee's evaluation, or corrects an employee when he is out of line, Don always begins by making it clear that he doesn't judge others negatively. Don is a scholar, a powerful teacher, and tremendously influential, but his greatest legacy is likely how he makes people feel when they interact with him. They feel that he genuinely wants to hear what they have to say, that he doesn't see himself as any better than them, that he sees their value as people. They feel that way because it is true. He does.

People love to talk with Don because his nonjudgmental way of communicating helps them feel safe and valued. Don recognizes, I believe, that judgment destroys equality and creates unsafe environments for conversations. If I judge you as having done something well or poorly, by doing that very act I put myself one-up and put you one-down. Michael Fullan has written about the importance of taking a nonjudgmental stance in many books, including *The Six Secrets of Change* (2008):

> Nonjudgmentalism is a secret of change because it is so very heavily nuanced. You have to hold a strong moral position without succumbing to moral superiority as your sole change strategy. As [William]

Miller puts it, "When we strive for some great good or oppose some great evil, it is extremely difficult not to spill out some of the goodness onto ourselves and the evil onto our opponents, creating a deep personal moral gulf. It is very difficult, in other words, professing or striving for something righteous, to avoid self-righteousness and moral condemnation." (p. 60)

Dennis and Michelle Reina in *Trust and Betrayal in the Workplace* (2006) have written about the importance of what they call "communication trust," which they define as "the willingness to share information, tell the truth, admit mistakes, maintain confidentiality, give and receive constructive feedback, and speak with good purpose" (p. 34). Conversational trust develops, they say, "when people feel comfortable and safe enough to share their perceptions regarding one another's perceptions without repercussions. They trust they will not suffer the consequences of retaliation because they spoke the truth" (p. 47). Passing judgment on others frequently destroys conversational trust.

> It's not our differences that divide us. It's our judgments about each other that do.
>
> — **Margaret Wheatley**
> (2009, p. 47)

To be nonjudgmental does not mean we ignore reality. Certainly, when we are engaged with the world and especially when we are in leadership positions, we need to use our ability to discern reality. Being nonjudgmental means we don't share our perceptions in a way that diminishes others. When we are nonjudgmental, we don't roll our eyes when we talk about another person. And as I heard Michael Fullan say in a presentation sometime back, "there are many ways we can roll our eyes that don't involve our eyes."

Belief 5: Conversation Should Be Back and Forth

Emily Manning is a district instructional coach in Denton, Texas, who volunteered to learn and practice Habit 3, Fostering Dialogue, for our study. She wrote on her reflection form that she was learning a lot about herself through our project, but she admitted that it was challenging for her to coach herself. "You have to be honest with yourself," she wrote, "and sometimes that's hard."

Emily read through the material on dialogue (see Chapter 4), and she said that the reading "really freed her up to be vulnerable and imperfect in a conversation. I can be a learner, too," she wrote. "I like that."

Emily watched video of herself in different conversations and realized, as many coaches do, that she needed to work on her questioning. "I sound like a broken record," Emily said,

> but I ask too many questions that are closed or that are "judgments in disguise." I need to scale back, especially when I am working with a first-year teacher that is seeking help. Too often I just want to go into teacher mode. I need to provide more space for us to construct together instead of me controlling the direction of the conversation. I think thoughtful questions that open dialogue will help.

Watching herself on video, Emily said, made her "more aware of my conversations . . . when I am overtaking a dialogue and when I'm more balanced. I'm also very aware of my questions now." To improve, Emily had to recognize first that she believed conversation should be back and forth, and then she had to practice her habits until she saw results. And, she did start to see results. Near the end of her experiment with dialogue, Emily wrote the following: "I was happy with this dialogue. I felt like at the end we had constructed a plan together, and it took both our thinking to get there."

Emily was practicing Habit 3, Fostering Dialogue, and in Chapter 4, I describe dialogue as a habit we can practice so we can have conversations where we think together with others. However, real dialogue is only possible if we embrace the belief that conversation should be back and forth. When we believe that meaning in conversations should be mutually constructed and not top-down, the habit of dialogue is possible.

A belief that conversation should be back and forth is almost inevitable if we adopt the other Better Conversations Beliefs. If I see others as equals, if I want to hear what they have to say, if I recognize that people are going to make their autonomous decisions about what I share, then inevitably I will assume that a better conversation is one that is created by everyone in the conversation. Seeing conversation as a two-way interaction is to live out our true respect for the

> The pulse of a strong relationship involves a rhythmic movement between giving and taking, talking and listening, valuing the other person and feeling commensurately valued in return.
>
> — Jim Loehr and Tony Schwartz
> (2003, p. 81)

people with whom we communicate. In fact, when we truly see others as complete human beings, and we respect them as autonomous people rather than objects to be manipulated, we almost always embrace back-and-forth interactions.

As one research volunteer wrote, a respectful, back-and-forth conversation about an important topic takes all of us thinking together "to get there." During a back-and-forth conversation, all parties are engaged and shaped by a free and honest discussion. In *On Dialogue* (1996), David Bohm provides a helpful analogy illustrating what such a conversation might actually look like. Bohm writes:

> The picture or image that this derivation suggests is of a *stream of meaning* flowing among and through us and between us . . . out of which will emerge some new understanding. It's something new, which may not have been in the starting point at all. It's something creative. And this *shared meaning* is the "glue" or "cement" that holds people and societies together. (p. 1, italics in original)

Belief 6: Conversation Should Be Life-Giving

While I was working on this chapter, I posted a simple question on our Facebook page, www.facebook.com/instructional.coaching. I asked the readers to describe someone they knew who was a great communicator. They did not disappoint me with their responses.

Tess Koning from Lismore Diocese, New South Wales, Australia, wrote about her supervisor and mentor, Tonia Flanagan. "Tonia saw in me, before I saw them, the qualities of a confident leader," Tess wrote.

> She watched me in my roles and coached me by asking me questions that helped me discern without leading me. She listened to my fears, encouraged me to take risks and persevere. I loved her term for having difficult conversations with staff as "open to learning" conversations. I think she is the epitome of what women can bring to leadership, communicating through understanding people at a more emotional level.

Denise Sheehan, from Canberra, Australia, wrote about her former secondary school coordinator, Jack Shannon, who "always listens, always smiles, always is calm." Denise wrote about one occasion, when

> a primary school teacher asked if a high school student being sent to the primary to do jobs is "a good kid." Jack smiled and responded, "all our kids are good kids." In short, Jack never imposes, is focused on the positive, and encourages the positive. . . . and we still get the lesson behind what he says.

Marty Conrad from Lander, Wyoming, wrote about a Northern Arapaho elder, the late Pius Moss, with whom he team taught at St. Stephens Indian Mission in Wyoming during the 1980s. Marty wrote, "Pius Moss would always indicate every day to me and everyone that 'It was a good day' no matter what the weather was . . . even at 25 below zero. . . . *every day* was a good day!!"

What struck me about all of the comments on the Facebook page was the people who were identified sounded like people with whom anyone would love to talk. Lou Ring Sangdahl, for example, described her neighbor who, she wrote, "is genuinely interested in other people, always learning, always quick to make connections, and always quick to share what is positive about other people." The other people who were described listened, asked questions that made people think, were engaged, positive, encouraging, and saw the good in others. They weren't going through the motions—they really cared about other people and they communicated that they respected them. They believed, whether they realized it or not, that conversations should be life-giving.

When I believe conversations should be life-giving, I go into conversations expecting that my conversation partners and I will leave conversations feeling more alive for having experienced them. People usually feel better when they engage in conversations about topics that matter, and when their ideas are heard and acted upon. Furthermore, when people come together to set and achieve goals, a real bond can develop, a deep affection can grow, and important life-long friendships can take root.

Michelle Harris was an instructional coach on our study of coaching in Beaverton, Oregon. When I interviewed her for my book *Focus on Teaching: Using Video for High-Impact Instruction* (2014), she told me that one of the best outcomes of participating was the relationships she developed with the other members of the Video Learning Team, Lea Molzcan, Jenny MacMillan, and Susan Leyden. "There is a bond that I share with everyone in that group that I don't share with anyone else," she said, adding . . .

> Human conversation is the most ancient and easiest way to cultivate the conditions for change—personal change, community and organizational change, planetary change. If we can sit together and talk about what's important to us, we begin to come alive.
>
> **—Margaret Wheatley**
> (2002, p. 3)

Having video to review and talk about took everything deeper. You're talking about what you are doing as a person, and it's like therapy. We really hammered through some personal and philosophical thoughts. I know that if I ever, ever had some sort of conundrum or dilemma related to work I could call on any of these women and they would listen to me and try to help or coach me. We still get together every single month to catch up and talk about work.

Every so often we have conversations that touch us so deeply and so positively that they actually change our lives. During those interactions, we are almost always deeply engaged in what is being said. When we care about what others say and respect others as equals, we are more likely to find ourselves talking about important topics, and conversations about what matters are often life-giving.

When those we talk with hear what we are saying, when we think together with others about important topics, and when we feel affirmed by those with whom we talk, we usually feel energized. At their best, conversations help us better understand what matters, what we need to do, and why we are the right person for doing what needs to be done—and that usually means we are more enthusiastic about taking on whatever challenge life brings us.

Revisiting Jane and Her Supervisor

How would Jane's conversation with her supervisor, mentioned at the beginning of this chapter, have been different if Jane's supervisor had adopted the beliefs inherent in better conversations? He would have seen Jane as an equal deserving respect and acknowledgment as a professional. He would have listened to Jane in a nonjudgmental way, perhaps starting the conversation by ensuring he understood

Jane's perspective on her school. The supervisor would have tried to create a setting for the conversation where he and Jane could discuss the school collaboratively. He would have shared his opinions and concerns clearly, but he would have shared them in a way that encouraged Jane to reciprocate and share her opinions and concerns just as clearly. He would have encouraged Jane to talk because he truly believed she would have something worthwhile to share.

Through the back-and-forth flow of conversation, the supervisor would have striven for a mutually constructed solution, encouraging Jane to share her thoughts and ideas about next steps for her school. If he truly embraced the Better Conversations Beliefs, he would not have been satisfied with the conversation unless both he and Jane left the conversation empowered and committed to moving forward positively. He would have been committed to having conversations that made life better.

TO SUM UP

Knowing what we believe about conversations is important because when our beliefs are inconsistent with our actions, people might rightfully question our authenticity. Six beliefs have been identified as foundational to the Better Conversation approach to interaction. Those beliefs are the following:

1. **I see conversation partners as equals** means that we do not see ourselves as better than others and our way of interacting shows that we see the value in other people.

2. **I want to hear what others have to say** means that we see conversation as an opportunity to learn others' ideas and hear about their experiences.

3. **I believe people should have a lot of autonomy** means we recognize that (a) not giving choice frequently engenders resistance, and (b) since we define who we are by the choices we make, taking away choice is dehumanizing.

4. **I don't judge others** means that when I interact or observe, I resist the temptation to diminish others

through critical judgments. When we judge others, we put ourselves one-up and put them one-down.

5. **I believe conversation should be back and forth** means I go into conversations with humility, open to learning, and ready to discover that I might be wrong. When I embrace this belief, I don't silence myself, but I speak in a way that makes it easy for others to say what they think.

6. **I believe conversation should be life-giving** means that I expect conversation to be energizing, affirmative, and generative. I usually should feel better after having had a better conversation.

GOING DEEPER

I could not have written this book without the research and thoughts of people like Michael Fullan, David Bohm, Edgar Schein, Margaret Wheatley, Peter Block, and Paulo Freire. Since those authors are mentioned in other parts of this book, I won't write more about them here—but to get a deeper understanding of the beliefs behind better conversations, readers would be wise to read their works with care.

If you are a leader in any capacity (and just about everyone in a school is a leader), I suggest you take time to understand Edward Deci and Richard Ryan's Self-Determination Theory (SDT). Their website, selfdetermina tiontheory.org, provides many accessible articles that will give you an overview of their work, and in my opinion Deci and Ryan's *Why We Do What We Do: Understanding Self-Motivation* (1995) should be required reading for anyone who leads in any way.

I was so impressed by Robert Sutton's *Good Boss, Bad Boss: How to Be the Best . . . and Learn From the Worst* (2010) when it came out that I wrote a series of columns on my blog, radicallearners.com, about how his ideas of leadership apply in the classroom. Sutton has written many helpful books, and I'm especially grateful for his insights into how power corrupts our ability to communicate with empathy.

Shane Lopez's *Making Hope Happen: Create the Future You Want for Yourself and Others* (2013) is the best book on hope that I have found. Shane is a smart, charming, funny person, and his research-based, accessible book gives us a language and stories for understanding and talking about hope. Shane's research on voice and engagement in schools is extremely important, and you can find some of his key studies simply by searching the Internet for "Shane Lopez, Gallup, Engagement."

Finally, speaking of better conversations, I am grateful for every chance I get to talk with Russ Quaglia, who wrote *Student Voice: The Instrument of Change* (2014) with Michael J. Corso. Russ is always engaged, always provocative, and always fun, and his book should be read by anyone who spends time with children in any capacity. His simple, radical idea—that students should have a real voice in their learning—needs to be given careful attention by educators and policy makers.

Listening With Empathy

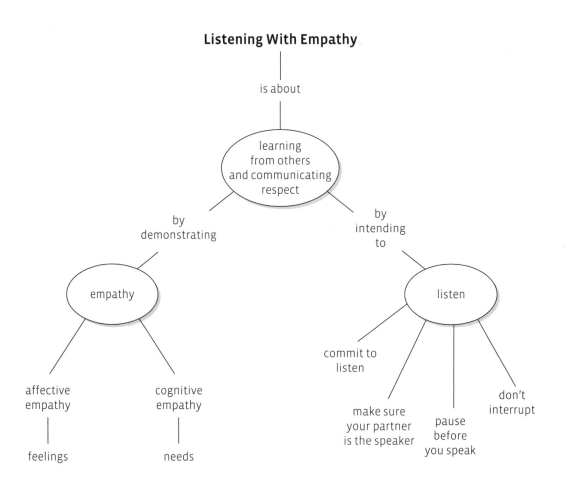

is about

learning
from others
and communicating
respect

by
demonstrating

by
intending
to

empathy

listen

affective
empathy

cognitive
empathy

commit to
listen

feelings

needs

make sure
your partner
is the speaker

pause
before
you speak

don't
interrupt

LISTENING WITH EMPATHY

Empathy withers and dies when we fail to acknowledge the humanity of other people—their individuality and uniqueness—and treat them as beings of less than equal worth to ourselves.

—Roman Krznaric (2014, p. 75)

I always thought of listening as something passive and too slow . . . something that happens as you formulate what next to say. Now I see listening as an art form—a lost way of communicating our humanity and kindness.

—Maria Furgiuele,
Teacher, Saskatchewan, Canada

Demonstrating Empathy

It is not by chance that the first habit in this book is demonstrating empathy. So much of communication, whether we are presenting to a large audience or consoling a three-year-old, depends on our ability to understand what our conversation partners think and feel. Before we design a beautiful slide or ask a probing question, our first thought should be, "What are my conversation partners thinking and feeling about this topic?"

We demonstrate empathy by using our imagination to see the world through others' eyes and feel the world through others' hearts. One example of empathy is described by Alexis Wiggins in a column published on her father Grant Wiggins' blog.[1] In her column, Alexis described how she experienced empathy by shadowing students for two days to see what it would be like to "be" a student.

"My task," she wrote, "was to do everything the student was supposed to do: If there was lecture or notes on the board, I copied them as fast as I could into my notebook. If there was a chemistry lab, I did it with my host student. If there was a test, I took it. The experience," she wrote, "was so eye-opening that I wish I could go back to every class of students I ever had right now and change a minimum of ten things—the layout, the lesson plan, the checks for understanding. Most of it!"

Alexis identified three insights. First, "students sit all day, and sitting is exhausting . . . I could not believe how tired I was after the first day . . . We forget as teachers, because we are on our feet a lot . . . But students," she wrote, "move almost never. And never is exhausting."

Her second insight was that students sit passively and listen "during approximately 90% of their classes." The teacher wrote, "It was not just the sitting that was draining but that so much of the day was spent absorbing information, but not often grappling with it. I was struck," she continued, "by . . . how little of their learning they are directing or choosing."

Alexis' third insight was that "you feel a little bit like a nuisance all day long. There was a great deal of sarcasm and snark directed at students, and I recognized, uncomfortably, how much I myself had engaged in this kind of communication." As a teacher, she knew how frustrating it can be to "have to explain things five times," but when she was a student, she saw things differently. "I was stressed. I was anxious. I had questions. And if the person teaching answered those questions by rolling their eyes at me, I would never want to ask another question again. I feel a great deal more empathy for students," she wrote, "after shadowing, and I realize that sarcasm, impatience, and annoyance are a way of creating a barrier between me and them. They do not help learning."

---

[1]https://grantwiggins.wordpress.com/2014/10/10/a-veteran-teacher-turned-coach-shadows-2-students-for-2-days-a-sobering-lesson-learned/

There is a good chance you have read this blog because it became a viral sensation, getting more than 1,000,000 hits since the year it was published. No doubt people were drawn to the column because they were interested in the ideas the writer shared, but I also think they read it because it so clearly illustrated the power of empathy. People saw that by understanding others, they could learn to be better.

Alexis' experience is an example of one way we can demonstrate empathy in our schools, but there are many other ways. What if professional developers spent two days understanding everything teachers face by shadowing teachers? What if teachers spent two days learning everything their principals or superintendents face by shadowing them? What if a governor, intent on cutting funding for special education classes, spent a day teaching a middle school class of 20 students who have been diagnosed as having severe emotional disorders, and then spent another day following one of the students from the class?

Demonstrating empathy, despite its importance, is not very highly valued today. Frequently, people are reduced to stereotypes, and whole groups of people are labeled based on politics, gender, race, religion, sports preferences, or even the type of smartphones they use. When we reduce people to types, we stop seeing them as the unique people they are and start to see them as categories with common—usually negative—traits; for example, all conservatives are only concerned with themselves, all Yankee fans are arrogant, and all Apple users are sheep doing whatever Apple wants them to do. Those stereotypes become much worse and more destructive when people start to talk about gender, race, or religion.

We can even embrace stereotypes as we reject them. For example, left-minded people can stereotype all right-minded people as narrow-minded at the very moment when they argue against stereotyping based on race, and right-minded people can label all left-minded people as immoral at the very moment they argue that the unique freedom of each individual must be respected. The way to fight for equality, or freedom, or respect is to see all people as fully human, not to dehumanize them by reducing them to a stereotype. And the way to do that is by demonstrating empathy.

In his book *Empathy: Why It Matters, and How to Get It* (2014), Roman Krznaric elaborates on the meaning of empathy:

> [E]mpathy is the art of stepping imaginatively into the shoes of another person, understanding their feelings and perspectives, and using that understanding to guide your actions. So empathy is distinct from expressions of sympathy—such as pity or feeling sorry for somebody—because these do not involve trying to understand the other person's emotions or point of view. (p. 8)

When we really understand people, we see them differently, and our broader understanding of them creates the opportunity for better conversations. We see others as people instead of objects. Martin Buber explains this distinction in *I and Thou* (1970). Buber refers to the objectification of others as "I-It." As Daniel Goleman (2006) has written, "Buber coined the term 'I-It' for the range of relations that runs from merely detached to utterly exploitative. In that spectrum, others become objects: we treat someone more as a thing than as a person" (p. 105). Goleman offers an anecdote that captures how it can feel when we experience an I-It conversation:

> A woman whose sister had recently died got a sympathy call from a male friend who had lost his own sister a few years before. The friend expressed condolences, and the woman, touched by his empathic words, told him poignant details of the long illness her sister had suffered, and she described how bereft she herself felt at the loss.
>
> But as she talked, she could hear the clicking of computer keys at the other end of the line. A slow realization dawned: her friend was answering his email, even as he was talking to her in her hour of pain. His comments became increasingly hollow, perfunctory, and off point as the conversation continued.
>
> After they hung up, she felt so dejected that she wished he had never called at all. She'd just had a gut punch of the interaction that the philosopher Martin Buber called "I-It." (p. 105)

One starting point for empathy is to see people as subjects rather than objects. This requires thinking carefully about how we see others. One major challenge may be that we simply do not want to hear what others are saying. We are usually drawn to those messages that confirm our hopes or affirm our assumptions about ourselves. Even after years of communication training, for example, many find it easier to listen to praise than criticism. David Bohm in *On Dialogue* (1996) describes what can happen when someone examines the way they listen:

> If one is alert and attentive, he can see, for example, that whenever certain questions arise, there are fleeting questions of fear, which push him away from consideration of these questions and of pleasure, which attract his thoughts and cause them to be occupied with other questions . . . can each of us be aware of the subtle fear and pleasure sensations that block his ability to listen freely? Without this awareness, the injunction to listen to the whole of what is said will have little meaning. (p. 5)

We struggle to listen with empathy because our ways of making sense of events can interfere with our ability to see the world as it is. For example, an instructional coach from an eastern part of the United States wrote about how her personal experiences with others could interfere with her ability to listen. After she left a meeting frustrated with how she interacted with others, she wrote, "I really need to not try to figure out motives of people and instead just think about what they are saying."

Many volunteers who participated in our global communication study wrote about how they find it much easier to understand people they like compared with people they don't like. A coach in Singapore wrote, "I had to remind myself that what the other person said was important, even if I don't like his personality. I need to remind myself that his words are important, and since we work in the same place, I have to learn to understand what he says."

In *Crucial Conversations: Tools for Talking When Stakes Are High* (2002), Kerry Patterson, Joseph Greeny, Ron McMillan, and Al Switzler describe how the "clever stories" we tell can

Empathy is the very means by which we create social life and advance civilization.

—Jeremy Rifkin
(2009, p. 10)

interfere with our ability to demonstrate empathy. One way we do this is to tell ourselves that someone else is fully responsible for the problems or difficulties we experience, and furthermore they are doing this because they have some character flaw—they are selfish, insensitive, bull-headed. Patterson and his colleagues call this a villain story. When we adopt a villain story, it can obscure our vision of reality.

One volunteer in our study, a professional developer from the United States, wrote about a group of teachers who saw her as the villain. "I was talking about growth and fixed mindset," she wrote, "and they thought I was telling them they had a fixed mindset. As a result, they completely stopped listening and rejected everything I said." If we are not mindful, all of us can slip into adopting a clever story in trivial or important ways—whether we are upset at the slow driver in the passing lane or the teacher who tells us what we don't want to hear about our son or daughter.

A second type of clever story that Patterson and his colleagues describe is the helpless story. Here, we create a story in which we convince ourselves that we are helpless in the face of some challenge. Patterson's ideas about "clever stories" are similar to what Martin Seligman (2006) wrote about learned helplessness and optimism and Carol Dweck (2006) has written about fixed and growth mindsets. We can tell ourselves that there is nothing we can do to change a situation that is affecting our lives even when there might be a great deal that we could do.

A helpless story in schools is the belief there is nothing we can do to teach students who aren't motivated, or whose parents don't care, or when we have too much paperwork, and so forth. It is easy to be seduced by such stories because teaching can be overwhelming. However, when we adopt a story, we stop seeing students as individuals and unconsciously start to look for evidence to support our story. As with villain stories, helpless stories interfere with our ability to see reality clearly, and most troubling, they make it difficult for us to see the unique attributes of each human being who sits in a staff meeting or classroom.

We can counteract our clever stories by first clearing our minds of the thoughts that might make it difficult for us to demonstrate empathy. I learned this from a coach of coaches when we discussed her attempt at empathy. Maureen tried to be empathetic with family members during conversations about the kind of care her 90-year-old father-in-law should receive. "I had a hard time listening," Maureen told me, "because I had a lot of baggage in my mind from previous conversations. The only way I could understand their story was to get my story out of my head first."

Marshall B. Rosenberg, in *Nonviolent Communication: A Language of Life* (1990), refers to this clearing of the mind as empathy toward ourselves; that is, we need to understand our own thoughts and feelings before we can understand others. We can show empathy toward ourselves, Rosenberg writes,

> by listening to what's going on in ourselves with the same quality of presence and attention that we offer to others. Former United Nations Secretary-General Dag Hammarskjold once said, "The more faithfully you listen to the voice within you, the better you will hear what is happening outside." If we become skilled at giving ourselves empathy, we often experience in just a few seconds a natural release of energy that then enables us to be present with the other person. (p. 103)

Once we have demonstrated empathy toward ourselves, we can demonstrate empathy toward others. To do this, we need to understand that empathy, as Krznaric explains, is most commonly described as having two components— affective empathy and cognitive empathy. Affective empathy, Krznaric writes, "is about sharing or mirroring another person's emotions. So if I see my daughter crying in anguish and I too feel anguish, then I am experiencing affective empathy. If, on the other hand, I notice her anguish but feel a different emotion, such as pity ('Oh, the poor little thing,' I might think), then I am showing sympathy rather than empathy. Sympathy typically refers to an emotional response that is not shared" (2014, p. 11).

Cognitive empathy or perspective taking, Krznaric writes, "involves making an imaginative leap and recognizing that other people have different tastes, experiences, and world views than our own" (p. 10). One important part of cognitive empathy is to identify our own needs and our conversation partners' needs. As the following box illustrates, people's needs come in many shapes and sizes.

In order to listen, you have to be still. You have to quiet your inner self, and you have to be willing to be vulnerable to being changed by your conversation partner. You have to be willing to say to somebody, "Oh, man, I know how that feels, I've been there myself. Let's just walk through this together."

—Carol Walker,
Instructional Coach,
Green River,
Wyoming

This list is based on Marshall B. Rosenberg's List of Needs in *Non-Violent Communication: A Language of Life* (1990):

- **Autonomy:** goals, values, dreams, personal growth
- **Celebration:** births, birth dates, marriages, losses, milestone events
- **Integrity:** principles, self-awareness, learning, honesty, self-efficacy
- **Purpose:** contributions, meaning, self-worth, learning, creativity
- **Relationships:** psychological safety, respect, support, trust, understanding, love, validation, reassurance
- **Play:** fun, joy, laughter
- **Spiritual Communion:** silence, beauty, guidance, knowledge, inspiration, harmony, order
- **Physical Nurturance:** health, food, weather, rest, exercise, shelter, sexual expression, touch, rest

One of main points Roman Krznaric (2014) makes in *Empathy* is that there is ample evidence to show that empathy can be learned. We can "humanize our imagination" (p. 83), Krznaric says, by expanding our capacity for empathy: "There is overwhelming agreement among the experts that our personal empathy quota is not fixed: we can develop our empathic potential throughout our lives. Our brains are surprisingly malleable, or 'plastic,' enabling us to rewire our neural circuitry" (p. 55).

GETTING BETTER AT DEMONSTRATING EMPATHY

For this habit and the other ten habits in the book, I suggest three ways of getting better—*Looking Back, Looking At,* and *Looking Ahead*. When we Look Back, we consider interactions we've had with people in the past and think about how they proceeded and what we can learn from them so we can be more effective in the future. Schön (1991) refers to this as reflection on action.

When we Look At, we consider interactions we are having or observing. We might keep a log of times we demonstrate empathy, for example, or take notes on the ways others do or do not demonstrate empathy. Schön (1991) refers to this way of thinking as reflection in action.

Looking Ahead is making plans for how we will interact in the future. When we Look Ahead to demonstrate empathy, we consider our own thoughts and feelings and the thoughts and feelings of others. Killion and Todnem (1991) refer to this as reflection for practice. To genuinely internalize habits, we will likely have to Look Back, Look At, and Look Ahead several times, on our own, with coaches, or teams.

At the end of this chapter, there are forms that anyone can use to Look Back, Look At, and Look Ahead. Volunteers in our study reported that they found it most helpful to use video to Look Back at their conversations and to write their thoughts down on the reflection forms.

> If there's no empathy, there's no listening. You can be hearing things, but I don't think you can be listening unless you have empathy.
>
> **—Carol Walker,**
> Instructional Coach,
> Green River,
> Wyoming

Listening With Empathy

Carol Walker knows how important it is to listen. An instructional coach in Green River, Wyoming, for the past 12 years, and a secondary Spanish and English teacher for the previous 26, Carol was a participant in our global communication study. In my interview with Carol, she told me how important listening was for her work as a coach. "I don't think I can be an instructional coach unless I listen. Listening is how I learn from my conversation partners; how I support and cheer for them. Sometimes when I listen, I help people peel away things so they can see where their strengths are and where conflicts might be hiding."

"Listening," Carol says, "might be the most important tool for an instructional coach," but Carol sees listening as important in all aspects of life. For Carol, "listening is like oxygen. A healthy relationship simply cannot exist without it. When I listen, I allow the conversation to change me. Listening opens that door. But when I don't listen, the relationship becomes unhealthy—the transaction becomes tainted."

After years of teaching and coaching, Carol has learned that listening requires more of us than just not talking. In our interview, Carol said, "A lot of the time people confuse being silent with listening, but listening is more than holding silent. If people's souls have listening organs, they must use them when they are listening."

In order to become a better listener, Carol reads widely, and she told me she has learned a lot, especially from Brené Brown's books *The Gifts of Imperfection* and *Daring Greatly*, Mark Nepo's *Seven Thousand Ways to Listen*, and Don Miguel

Ruiz's *The Four Agreements* and *The Fifth Agreement*. For Carol, listening is a way of life, not just a communication skill, so she was very willing to record herself in a conversation and watch her video to see what she might learn.

Given how important listening is to Carol, it might not be surprising to discover that one of the conversations she wrote about for our study was one where she was disappointed by how she listened. When Carol reviewed her conversation, she saw that she focused more on how her partner communicated than what he communicated. Reflecting on her conversation, Carol wrote on her reflection form, "I am heartily disappointed that my own lack of connection with a topic can lead to a lack of connection with a person. I have a lot to work on. There needs to be much less of me when others need my ear."

WE STRUGGLE TO LISTEN

Most people recognize the importance of listening. Almost every communication, relationship, or leadership book identifies listening as essential. And yet, when participants in our global study watched themselves in conversation, what they usually first noticed about the way they communicated was that they needed to become better listeners. Kathy DeVillers reflected, "I always knew I was a quick talker and interrupter, but I never realized how much it affected my ability to really listen to what others were saying to me." When people watched their videos they usually found, as Rebecca Jenkins wrote, "I always underestimate how much I talk and over estimate how much I listen."

So what do good listeners do? In part, good listening should be the natural outgrowth of the Better Conversations Beliefs I wrote about in Chapter 1. If we see our conversation partners as equal partners, then conversation should be back and forth. If we truly want to hear what the other person has to say, then we should listen better. We should, but our global study of communication reveals that we do not always do what we think we do.

For that reason, we need to learn and practice a few simple habits so our actions embody our beliefs. If we reflect on our beliefs and act to master a few high-leverage habits, we can become better listeners and start to have better conversations. The strategies are simple. They can be mastered by anyone, and when they are applied with discipline, they will make you a much better listener, a more effective leader, and a better friend.

Strategy 1: Commit to Really Listen. The first listening strategy is a simple but absolutely vital one, to commit to hearing the other person. When we commit to listening, we enter into conversations determined to let the other person speak, and this means we don't fill up the conversation with our own words. This is easier said than done. One research volunteer wrote about how difficult it was for her to simply commit to letting her conversation partner speak:

> I was absolutely appalled at how many times I talked over my conversation partner. Everything I said was an agreement, and encouragement, etc., but it sounded so incredibly rude as I listened to it on the tape. I was surprised by how much I talked over the speaker. In my mind, I've been aware of this all along, but I have never stopped myself from doing it because my comments are always supportive and encouraging. Listening to myself doing this, however, was appalling. Rather than encouraging, it's just plain rude, and I wonder how others have put up with this.

One of the challenges with listening is that we often fail to recognize when we are not listening. Our electronic devices, in particular, can pull us away from a conversation in a microsecond. Many participants in our study confirmed that their technology made it harder to talk. Beth Madison wrote that "having an open laptop and even glancing at it while talking to someone else can be a conversation turn-off." One participant wrote that she had to teach herself to avoid distractions. "When someone wants to talk to me, I now get up and move away from my computer and desk. I find somewhere to sit where there are not many distractions."

Authentic listening is something we feel as much as we see. You can tell when your sister who lives 2,000 miles away isn't listening when you are talking with her on the phone. Clearly, you can feel when someone right besides you is or is not listening. Authentic listening causes a genuine connection between people. If you

I have learned that many people would like to have someone listen to them pretty much uninterrupted on any topic of their choice. I think this points out how much we crave personal time. Not many can afford private counseling, so inviting folks to sit down and have a chance to open up about some pressing topic is probably a good thing.

—Research volunteer

choose to make sure you are really listening to your partner, he or she will know. And so will you.

Strategy 2: Be the Listener, Not the Speaker. Good listeners give others plenty of opportunity to speak. For that reason, you should teach yourself to ask, "Am I the listener or am I the speaker?" If you find that you are always the speaker, work on taking on the alternate role.

There are many ways you can shift to being the listener. You can make a decision to care about what your partner has to say. You can also pose questions to the person you're talking with rather than telling him or her what you have to say. You can see every interaction as a chance to let the other person tell you something you don't know and see each conversation as a learning opportunity, not a telling opportunity. You can use questions to learn about your conversation partner. A great conversationalist lets the other person have the conversation.

As your conversation progresses, coach yourself by checking the situation and asking, "Am I the speaker, or am I the receiver?" If you're the speaker, then make a point to ask a question that hands the conversation back to your partner. Participants in our study had to use metacognitive strategies to keep the conversation focused on the other person. Michelle Gilbert wrote that she had to tell herself that "this person is speaking because they have a desire to be heard and they have something to say." Another volunteer wrote that she realized that "sometimes my mind is thinking about what I would do or what I think the Big Idea is, and I am not always right. I need to free my mind and just listen."

> I will be focusing on pausing and really thinking before responding. I keep going back to a comment—"see every interaction as a chance to let the other person tell you something you didn't know."
>
> —**Beth Madison,** Principal, Robert Gray Middle School, Portland, Oregon

Strategy 3: Pause and Think Before You Respond. Even if you listen with all your heart, mind, and soul, there is still a possibility that you will be perceived as a terrible listener. Careless words in response to what someone says can negate another person's comment and create the same impact as not listening at all. Let's say someone comes to me with a suggestion or idea, and without thinking, I quickly respond, "Oh, that will never work. We've tried that before, and it always fails." I may have heard what my colleague said, but my comment has the same impact as not listening because my words communicate that my partner's words had no impact on me at all.

A better strategy is to pause before responding and ask yourself, "Will what I'm about to say open up or close down the conversation?" If my comments shut down my partner, then I should find another way to respond—or say nothing. But, listening is more than taking words in. You may have had the experience where someone was able to parrot back what you said but who didn't really seem to listen to you. Listening is about hearing the words and being sure to process them. When we listen to others, we must make sure we let their words sink in, and then we need to comment in ways that authentically show we have heard what they have said. There are two techniques here, and both are important. First we pause, and second we think about what we will say before we speak.

When we pause, we allow for what I've heard Susan Scott, author of *Fierce Conversations*, describe in her presentations as the "sweet purity of silence." Learning to be quiet was an important skill for one research participant. She wrote that "silence is OK, even though it may be uncomfortable for a while. We have a tendency to fill the gap of silence."

A great description of the power of listening is provided by Marshall Goldsmith in his book *What Got You Here Won't Get You There* (2007). Goldsmith describes "one of his all-time heroes," Frances Hesselbein, who, Goldsmith tells us, was identified by Peter Drucker as "the finest executive he's ever known." Goldsmith writes:

> Frances Hesselbein does a lot of things well. But she does one thing superbly above all else. She thinks before she speaks. As a result, she is a world-class listener. If you asked her if this was a passive gesture, she would assure you that it requires great discipline, particularly when she is upset about what she is hearing. After all, what do most of us do when we're angry? We speak (and not in the carefully measured tones of a diplomat).
>
> What do we do when we're upset? We talk.
>
> What do we do when we're confused or surprised or shocked? Again, we talk. This is so predictable that we can see the other party almost cringe in anticipation of our harsh unthinking autoreflex response.
>
> Not so with Frances Hesselbein. You could tell her the world was about to end and she would think

> Listening stiches the world together. Because listening is the doorway to everything that matters. It enlivens the heart the way breathing enlivens the lungs. We listen to awaken our heart. We do this to stay vital and alive.
>
> —**Mark Nepo**
> (2013, p. xiv)

before opening her mouth, not only about what she would say but how she would phrase it.

Whereas most people think of listening as something we do during those moments *where we are not talking*, Frances Hesselbein knows that listening is a two-part maneuver. There's the part where we actually listen. And there's the part where we speak. Speaking establishes how we are perceived as a listener. What we say is proof of how well we listen. They are two sides of the same coin. (p. 148, italics in original)

Strategy 4: Don't Interrupt. If you find the first three strategies too difficult, there is a simple way you can improve your listening skills overnight. Stop interrupting other people when they are talking. When we interrupt others, we are showing them in not-so-subtle ways that we believe that what they are saying doesn't really matter—our comments matter so much more.

Listening is an important way to show respect for others. When we really listen, we have a chance to enter into a deeper form of communication. A conversation characterized by people really listening is humanizing for all parties. When we truly hear people, we see them as human beings who count, whose ideas, heart, and soul matter. When we interrupt, on the other hand, we treat others as objects put on earth only to help us get what we want. What's a good goal for how often we should interrupt? How about never?

> I am working on not interrupting others with my sense of urgency during many of my conversations with others and not formulating a response before the speaker is finished.
>
> **—Kathy DeVillers,**
> Professional Learning Specialist, Green Bay Area Public Schools, Wisconsin

GETTING BETTER AT LISTENING

There are many excellent books with great ideas about how to become a truly outstanding listener. To become an excellent listener, we need to demonstrate empathy, which as Roman Krznaric (2014) explains, involves understanding how others feel and what they are thinking (especially about their needs). Marshall Rosenberg (2003) writes that one powerful way to demonstrate empathy is by paraphrasing what we hear others saying. On her reflection forms for our global communication study, Joellen Killion, who has authored many helpful books about professional learning, stated that for her to be a good listener, she had to be careful not to let questions interfere with her ability to truly listen. Stephen Covey described the importance of listening as a way of understanding another's paradigm.

All of these ideas are outstanding, but I would suggest they represent the second level of listening. Once you are habitually listening to others, you should consider refining your habits by implementing these new practices. But the first task is simply to stop talking and hear what the other person says. Almost all of the participants who studied listening reported that they improved because they did not try to do too much. The four simple strategies— (a) commit to listen, (b) make sure your partner is the speaker, (c) pause before you speak and ask, "will my comment open up or close down this conversation?" and (d) don't interrupt—provided challenge enough. Once these strategies become habitual, you can move to level two, perhaps by reading some of the books described in the Going Deeper section.

You can get better at listening by internalizing the four simple strategies—either on your own or with a partner or team—by using the *Looking Back, Looking At,* or *Looking Ahead* reflection forms included at the end of this chapter.

The *Looking Back* form can be used to review conversations and assess your interest, how effectively you listened, and to identify what you can do to get better at listening.

The *Looking At* form can be used to consider models of good listening you see around you, to create your own understanding of what good listening is, and to identify strategies that you consider important for good listening.

The *Looking Ahead* form can be used to prepare yourself to truly hear what others are communicating and to move toward level two of listening by considering the emotions and needs your conversation partner might be feeling.

> **Effective Listening**
>
> 1. Commit to listen.
> 2. Make sure your partner is the speaker.
> 3. Pause before you speak and ask, "Will my comment open up or close down this conversation?"
> 4. Don't interrupt.

TO SUM UP

This book begins with the habit of demonstrating empathy because so much of communication depends on understanding others. When we demonstrate empathy, we see beyond our stereotypes and stop seeing people as objects. Instead, we start to see others as the unique subjects they are. Martin Buber (1970) referred to this as the distinction between "I-It."

Roman Krznaric (2014) identifies two components to empathy:

1. Affective empathy "is about sharing or mirroring another person's emotions."

2. Cognitive empathy "involves making an imaginative leap and recognizing that other people have different tastes, experiences, and world views than our own."

Marshall Rosenberg (2003) sees identifying others' needs as a crucial part of empathy.

Listening is one of the most important Better Conversations Habits, and when participants in our global study reviewed themselves on video, they almost always identified listening as an area where they wanted to get better.

If we embrace the Better Conversations Beliefs—especially that we see our conversation partners as equals, that conversation should be back and forth, and that we truly want to hear what the other person has to say—then we *should* listen with empathy. We should, but unfortunately that is not always the case. To be effective listeners, our habits need to be consistent with our beliefs.

In this chapter, four strategies are identified to promote the habit of effective listening:

1. Commit to listen.

2. Make sure your partner is the speaker.

3. Pause before you speak and ask, "Will my comment open up or close down this conversation?"

4. Don't interrupt.

GOING DEEPER

Roman Krznaric's *Empathy: Why It Matters, and How to Get It* (2014) is a great overview of writing about empathy. Krznaric draws on neuroscience research to argue that we are more than the self-interested beings described by authors such as Hobbes, Smith, Freud, and Dawkins. Krznaric provides useful definitions of empathy, especially when he distinguishes between cognitive and affective empathy. This is the book to read if you are interested in why empathy matters and how you can develop your own capacity for demonstrating it.

Krznaric acknowledges his debt, as I do, to Marshall B. Rosenberg's *Nonviolent Communication: A Language of Life* (2003), which almost lyrically describes the importance of empathy as a foundational support for meaningful human interaction. Rosenberg proposes that when we treat people like objects—that is, when we do not fully appreciate their humanity and need for freedom—we commit violence against them that can be even more damaging than physical violence. His book describes a theory of interaction grounded in the belief that everyone is capable of empathy, and it is through empathy or compassion that we can move beyond "right and wrong" conversations to more meaningful conversations that address our needs.

If you are interested in a scholarly articulation of the role of the theory of empathy in psychology, biology, the meaning of life, and ultimately the structure of society and implications for our future, see Jeremy Rifkin's hefty and impressive book *The Empathic Civilization: The Race to Global Consciousness in a World in Crisis* (2009). For an excellent introduction to the book, watch Alan Greg's interview of Rifkin on TVO (http://tvo.org/video/164754/jeremy-rifkin-empathic-civilization-full).

The book that first influenced my thinking about listening is Stephen Covey's classic work, *The 7 Habits of Highly Effective People,* first published in 1990. Like Dale Carnegie's *How to Win Friends and Influence People,* Covey's *7 Habits* is packed with wise advice for anyone who interacts with others, which is to say, everyone. Covey's advice to "seek first to understand, then be understood" remains excellent advice for people engaging in communication in the 21st century.

Marshall Goldsmith's short but powerful book *What Got You Here Won't Get You There* (2007) also offers excellent advice for communicators. Anyone who learns and takes to heart Goldsmith's 20 habits will be happier, more successful, and most likely a better person.

Mark Nepo's *Seven Thousand Ways to Listen* (2013), which Carol Walker described earlier in this book, defines listening as a way of life, not just a communication habit. The spiritual approach of the author won't appeal to everyone, but many consider this book to be essential reading for a well-lived life.

LOOKING BACK:

Demonstrating Empathy

Use this form to look back on a conversation where you attempted to demonstrate empathy. Try to identify what you did well, where you could improve, and what you should do differently during future conversations.

What assumptions or preconceptions (if any) did you bring to the conversation that made it difficult to listen with empathy?

In what way did your self-interests, opinions, judgments, or fears interfere with your ability to listen with empathy?

How well did you recognize the emotions your conversation partner was feeling?

How well did you perceive the spoken and unspoken needs your conversation partner had?

What should you do differently in the future do be more effective at demonstrating empathy?

LOOKING AT:

Demonstrating Empathy

Use this form to identify and note your comments about all the interactions you have with other people when you have stereotypical responses and you use your imagination to have more empathic responses. Use the spaces below to record your stereotypical response, your revised empathic response, and what you learned about yourself and others by choosing to see others with empathy.

Stereotypical Response

....

....

....

Empathic Response

....

....

....

Stereotypical Response

....

....

....

Empathic Response

....

....

....

Stereotypical Response

....

....

....

Empathic Response

....

....

....

What I Learned

....

....

....

....

LOOKING AHEAD:

Demonstrating Empathy

Use this form to prepare yourself for a conversation you are soon going to have where you intend to demonstrate empathy. Do your best to consider fully how you are thinking and feeling about the conversation, and how your conversation partner is thinking and feeling.

What assumptions or preconceptions are you bringing to the conversation that might make it difficult to listen with empathy?

What emotions do you anticipate your conversation partner might be feeling?

What needs do you think your conversation partner currently has regarding your future topic of conversation?

What other thoughts do you have about understanding your conversation partner's perspective and emotions?

LOOKING BACK:

Listening

Complete this form after you have recorded a conversation in which you tried to use the listening strategies. You can complete it while watching or after watching the conversation.

On a scale of 1-10, how interested were you in what the other person had to say?

Not Interested ○─○─○─○─○─○─○─○─○─○ Very Interested
 1 2 3 4 5 6 7 8 9 10

Is there anything you can do differently next time to be more invested in what your conversation partner has to say?

....

....

....

How many minutes were you the speaker or listener?

SPEAKER	LISTENER

Is there anything you can do differently next time to listen more?

....

....

....

What did you do that opened up or closed down the conversation?

....

....

....

Is there anything you can do differently next time to encourage your conversation partner to open up?

....

....

....

What else could you try to do differently next time to improve as a listener?

....

....

....

LOOKING AT:

Listening

//

What conversation did you observe to identify how people listen?

What was the topic of the conversation?

On a scale of 1-10, how well did people listen to each other?

Poor O—O—O—O—O—O—O—O—O—O Excellent
         1 2 3 4 5 6 7 8 9 10

What strategies or habits did you see people use that showed that they appeared to be listening?

How did people react when they were heard?

What strategies or habits did you see people use that showed that they appeared to be listening?

How did people react when they were not heard?

What did you learn about how you should listen to other people?

Listening

What is the conversation where you intend to practice listening with empathy?

_____

_____

_____

On a scale of 1-10, how interested do you expect to be in this conversation?

Poor O—O—O—O—O—O—O—O—O—O Excellent
　　　　1　2　3　4　5　6　7　8　9　10

On a scale of 1-10, how committed are you to listening with empathy?

Poor O—O—O—O—O—O—O—O—O—O Excellent
　　　　1　2　3　4　5　6　7　8　9　10

What can you do to increase your interest and commitment?

_____

_____

_____

What can you do to ensure that the focus of the conversation is on others rather than yourself?

_____

_____

_____

Have you cleared your mind? Is there anything else you need to do to make sure you are ready to listen without preconceptions and with empathy?

_____

_____

_____

What can you do to make sure you focus on the emotions and needs of others?

_____

_____

_____

_____

Fostering Dialogue

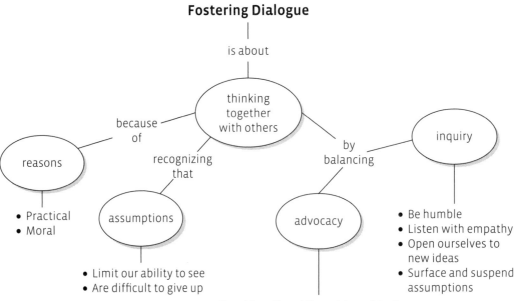

is about

thinking together with others

because of

reasons

recognizing that

by balancing

inquiry

- Practical
- Moral

assumptions

advocacy

- Be humble
- Listen with empathy
- Open ourselves to new ideas
- Surface and suspend assumptions

- Limit our ability to see
- Are difficult to give up

- Consider others' thoughts and feelings
- Clarify the meaning of words and concepts
- Provide contextual information
- Identify false assumptions
- Use stories

FOSTERING DIALOGUE

Dialogue . . . is a way of taking the energy of our differences and channeling it toward something that has never been created before. It lifts us out of polarization and into a greater common sense, and is thereby a means for accessing the intelligence and coordinated power of groups of people.

—William Isaacs (1999, p. 19)

There was one moment in the conversation where we created a task for students together using her ideas and it was beautiful. I need more of those moments.

—Emily Manning,
District Instructional Coach, Denton, Texas

Jennifer was an instructional coach in an elementary school in Northern California. For our global communication study, she experimented with Habit 3, Fostering Dialogue. Jennifer read the materials for our project, and then she went deeper, reading David Bohm's essay *On Dialogue*. "The book was fabulous for me," she said, "helping me understand my thought process and how everything connected."

To foster dialogue, Jennifer had to change the way she interacted with others. She committed to withholding judgment, suspending assumptions, asking questions, and listening with empathy rather than telling. She wanted to embrace dialogue by making sure her own thoughts and words didn't get in the way. She also video recorded her conversations to get a different perspective on how she was doing.

The first teacher who agreed to collaborate with Jennifer was a third-grade teacher with nearly 40 years' experience. At first, the teacher wasn't that interested in coaching; she'd invited Jennifer into to her class for a model lesson once, but that was about it. However, she agreed to collaborate when Jennifer told her about the dialogue experiment.

When they met to talk, they started their conversation by looking at student work and talking about one student in particular who was struggling to see the difference between informational and persuasive writing. To foster dialogue, Jennifer was intent to make no assumptions about her colleague's comments but to simply listen and validate her partner. "I noticed in my head that I kept wanting to make judgments, and I had to tell myself, 'don't go there!' I focused on respecting her opinions and asking questions that would help her talk about her assumptions and what she was thinking about this student in particular. That," Jennifer said, "worked lovely."

In her interview with me, Jennifer said,

I tried to more intentionally paraphrase what she was saying while also asking questions at a deeper level. The principles of dialogue are so simple. Respect them. Be willing to talk about what they are thinking. Maybe help them consider new ways of thinking. It was really delightful.

Jennifer wrote,

Dialogue really helped me live out the respect that I have toward this woman in a tangible way. Her body language softened during the conversation, and at one point tears filled her eyes, sighs of relief seemed evident, and she hugged me as I left, asking me to come again! I'm not sure it gets much better than that!

As a result of their conversation, Jennifer's teacher came up with a new way to motivate her student, and soon after, she emailed Jennifer to tell her the strategy had worked: "Getting the student to write about something that really mattered to him invoked this huge emotion in him and got him to understand why his writing needed to be more focused on something that he could support with evidence." Soon after, the teacher invited Jennifer to her classroom to see the students' writing and the passion they were writing with. "It was so much fun to see that," Jennifer wrote, "because it was something we figured out together."

Jennifer's teacher continued to grow. She started to see how other kids could benefit from having more of a voice in their learning, and Jennifer told me, the teacher's "excitement kind of took over the whole class after we did this." This conversation along with others Jennifer had with teachers "really showed the power of dialogue." What surprised Jennifer was that although the habit of fostering dialogue helped her be more effective as an instructional coach, the biggest impact was on her personal life. Jennifer told me when I interviewed her:

> It is because of dialogue that I understand my husband in a new way. We have been married for 34 years and actually gone through a lot of therapy. For me personally, this has been the first kind of Aha! where I realize what I need to work on. I now know I have to change the stories I have told myself for years. I have to suspend judgment and be a reflective partner to my husband. Personally, I feel like I have grown tremendously. Even in friendships, I realize there are things I need to let go of. So it has been a huge life changer for me. I'm starting to see people as partners, not projects.

What Is Dialogue?

The life change Jennifer experienced was a shift from a top-down approach to communication to a dialogue, and such a shift truly can be life changing. In traditional top-down conversations, the goal is usually to make sure messages are clearly communicated and received—people try to clearly explain their ideas and then try to persuade others to buy-in to what they explain. This is the opposite of a dialogue.

The goal of dialogue, as Jennifer's story illustrates, is to have a conversation where all parties understand, hear, shape, and are shaped by each other's thoughts. Consequently, a dialogue is a learning conversation. As we will explore,

The kind of conversation I'm interested in is one in which you start with a willingness to emerge a slightly different person. It is always an experiment, whose results are never guaranteed. It involves risk. It's an adventure in which we agree to cook the world together to make it taste less bitter.

—Theodore Zeldin
(1998, p. 3)

there are practical and moral reasons for adopting the habit of fostering dialogue.

PRACTICAL REASONS FOR FOSTERING DIALOGUE

Dialogical conversations are better conversations because they lead to better outcomes. Traditional top-down conversations result in one of two things, and neither promotes learning. First, top-down conversations can be active or passive power struggles where different participants try to impose their ideas onto the rest of the group. During active power struggles, two or more people fight it out, so to speak, trying to persuade others through their rhetoric and strength of conviction that they have the right idea and that others should adopt their idea. David Bohm, whose essay *On Dialogue* (1996) is a seminal document in the history of ideas about dialogue, describes this kind of conversation as being like a ping-pong game, "where people are batting the ideas back and forth and the object of the game is to win or to get points for yourself" (p. 7).

During passive power struggles, people simply surrender to the loudest or strongest voice without fighting. This often happens when one person has more power than others, such as when a principal and teacher discuss the teacher's evaluation. Often, passive power struggles are conversations that are endured and quickly forgotten. The person at the end of the top-down conversation nonverbally communicates that he understands and agrees, but inside he knows he doesn't plan to do what he is being told to do.

Top-down conversations also fail to produce results when participants focus on avoiding conflict rather than speaking the truth. During conflict-avoidance conversations, participants recognize that conflict might lead to hard feelings, so they spend more time keeping conflict at bay than they do saying what they think. When people say anything that might be slightly contradictory, they share their ideas tentatively or more often keep their thoughts to themselves.

Everyone in conflict-avoidance conversations works to keep surface harmony, even though, at the same time, they may also feel frustrated that they are unable to say what they think. At their worst, conflict-avoidance conversations, whether one-to-one or in groups, are frustrating and boring since people do not feel comfortable speaking up. If you find yourself feeling bored and disengaged during a conversation, chances are you are experiencing a conflict-avoidance conversation; people you're talking with are likely counting the seconds until it is over.

A dialogue is a better conversation. During dialogue, participants listen with empathy, and they respect and encourage others' views. Consequently, during dialogue people say what they think, but they do it in a way that encourages open rather than closed conversation. William Isaacs, in *Dialogue and the Art of Thinking Together* (1999), provides a simple question we can ask to see if we are experiencing dialogue: "Is there energy, possibility, and safety here?" (p. 244). If not, we are probably not experiencing dialogue.

MORAL REASONS FOR DIALOGUE

There are clear benefits when groups of two or more people come together and learn how to think together. As Peter Senge wrote in *The Fifth Discipline: The Art and Practice of The Learning Organization* (1990), when we embrace dialogue, "collectively, we can be more insightful, more intelligent than we can possibly be individually. The IQ of the team can potentially be much greater than the IQ of the individuals" (p. 239). There are obvious practical reasons for engaging in dialogue, but perhaps even more compelling are the moral reasons for dialogue.

The fundamental problem with traditional top-down models of communication is they always involve people imposing their messages onto others. Consequently, during top-down conversations, some people never get to speak. When we silence other people—as Martin Buber, Paulo Freire, David Bohm, and many others have explained—we fail to recognize them as fully alive, complete human beings. A top-down conversation turns others into objects, things—receptacles for our ideas, not partners. This is why, Bohm (1996) writes, "If somebody doesn't listen to your basic assumptions you feel it as an act of violence" (p. 53).

Dialogue involves respecting others and seeing them and their ideas as legitimate and responds to our universal, profound longing to be heard, to be validated, and to feel connected with others. Top-down conversation divides us, but dialogue, because it involves real listening and open,

> When dialogue is done skillfully, the results can be extraordinary: longstanding stereotypes dissolved, mistrust overcome, mutual understanding achieved, visions shaped and grounded in shared purpose, people previously at odds with one another aligned on objectives and strategies, new common ground discovered, new perspectives and insights gained, new levels of creativity stimulated, and bonds of community strengthened.
>
> **—Daniel Yankelovich**
> (1999, p. 16)

I think the biggest success I have encountered while working on dialogue is the joy I have found in having great dialogue with another person. I usually went into conversations with "the desire to be right" attitude. Growing up in a military family and having three brothers, I think I felt like I had to prove everything I believed in or wanted to do. Taking a step out of my selfishness in communicating and truly focusing on being humble, suspending the assumption that my way was the right way and genuinely listening to the person made the dialogue go smoothly, and I wasn't thinking of the next thing I was going to say as I was listening. I really felt like I built trust approaching the dialogue in this way.

—**Nicole Patton,**
Instructional
Coach, Heartland
AEA, Johnston, Iowa

creative conversation about topics that matter, unites us. For these reasons, Paulo Freire (1970) writes that "dialogue is an existential necessity" (p. 77).

Top-down communication not only dehumanizes those who are silenced, but it is also dehumanizes those who win conversations. People may get their way, but because they don't know what others think and feel, they miss the chance to connect with them. Top-down communication isolates the winners as much as it isolates the losers. Paulo Freire refers to dialogue as a mutually humanizing conversation. Top-down conversations, then, can be understood as mutually dehumanizing.

Why Dialogue Is Difficult

Since dialogue builds relationships and improves thinking, why isn't it a more common form of interaction? The answer is simple: Dialogue is not easy to foster. We fall prey to the habit of top-down communication in large part because it appears to be easier. The only problem is that it is also usually unsuccessful. With some effort we can adopt the habit of dialogue, but to do this, we have to understand what we are up against.

One reason why dialogue is difficult is that we are entrapped by our taken-for-granted assumptions and opinions about reality.

Bohm (1996) explains:

Everybody has different assumptions and opinions. They are basic assumptions—not merely superficial assumptions—such as assumptions about the meaning of life; about your own self-interest, your country's interest, or your religious interest; about what you really think is important . . . And these assumptions are defended when they are challenged. People frequently can't resist defending them, and they tend to defend them with an emotional charge. (p. 8)

Our assumptions make a mess of communication for at least two reasons. First, we interpret what others communicate through our assumptions, and that interferes with our ability to listen. I see this in conversations about best teaching practices all the time. For example, if one teacher works from the assumption that teaching should be constructivist and another works from the assumption that teaching should involve direct instruction, the two teachers might struggle to come to a shared meaning about what is best for students. Real dialogue, then, is only possible when people surface and critically analyze their assumptions.

The second issue is that people, often unconsciously, hold on to their assumptions very tightly. Our assumptions can provide us with a worldview, a sense of right and wrong, and a way of making sense of our professional and personal lives. Often our assumptions are tightly tied to our life's work, our loyalty to other people, and our spiritual or etymological beliefs. For that reason, when our assumptions are challenged, our beliefs about friends, work, right and wrong, God, our very existence seem threatened. No wonder people bristle when they are asked to rethink their assumptions.

Consider a classic, complex interaction: conversation during Thanksgiving dinner in the United States. Since our assumptions are tied to emotions and moral perspectives on life, a simple topic like gun control can touch on people's beliefs about freedom, patriotism, and God—and bring the whole dinner table discussion to a crashing halt. Some topics can be so uncomfortable that they simply become undiscussable. And yet, as David Bohm (1996) writes, "Love will go away if we can't communicate and share meaning" (p. 41). Adopting the habit of fostering dialogue is not easy, but it is essential.

How to Foster Dialogue

A dialogue is a back-and-forth conversation during which all members of the conversation hear and learn what others are saying and where all members share what they are thinking. A dialogue is much more than simply taking in information. In fact, if all we do is listen to others—and there are certainly times when that is what we should do—we are not engaging in dialogue. In a dialogue, all participants are actively involved in creating meaning and thinking together. All participants hear and understand what others have to say, and they also clearly share what is on their minds. As Chris Argyris has explained in *Action Science* (Argyris, Putnam, & Smith, 1985), dialogue involves equal parts advocacy and inquiry.

Emily Manning, who participated in our global communication study, wrote on her reflection forms that the project helped her become more aware of how she balances conversation during dialogue. "I notice," she wrote, "when I'm overtaking a dialogue and when I'm more balanced. Thoughtful questions that open dialogue are helpful."

ADVOCACY

People cannot "think together" with us if they do not understand what we are thinking and saying, so to engage in meaningful dialogue, we must clearly articulate and advocate for our ideas. There are at least five strategies we can employ to do this: (1) consider others' thoughts and feelings, (2) clarify the meaning of words and concepts, (3) provide contextual information others need so they can understand what we are sharing, (4) identify our false assumptions, and (5) use stories and analogies to help ideas come to life.

Consider Others' Thoughts and Feelings. When we understand our conversation partners' thoughts and feelings, we have a much greater chance of communicating clearly because we can position what we say in a way that responds to our partners' major concerns. For this reason, Habit 1, Demonstrating Empathy, is an important part of advocating for our perspective. One of the first thoughts we ask when we are communicating should always be, "What are others' needs and emotions with respect to our topic?"

Clarify the Meaning of Words and Concepts. As I write this, I am a father of a two-year-old, and it is one of the great joys of my life to watch and listen as Luke learns to talk. Just a few weeks back, Luke, riding his little tricycle, turned to me and spoke his first sentence: "Watch this, Dad!" Each new word and phrase opens up the world more and more to Luke, and language is helping him describe what he sees, wants, and doesn't want. And Luke's use of language makes it easier and easier for him and me to actually talk about

I am carrying these practices into conversations I have with my children, which is really making for some great conversations with them. When I talk to them and not judge what they say and truly listen and treat them as equals in the conversation, I find that they share more with me. I love the quote from David Bohm, "Love will go away if we can't communicate, and share meaning. . . . However, if we really communicate, then we will have fellowship, participation, friendship, love, growing and growth."

—**Nicole Patton,**
Instructional Coach, Heartland AEA, Johnston, Iowa

what is going on in his mind. The more words that Luke and I both understand, the more we communicate.

The same is true for communication between adults. Words are imperfect, and miscommunication often arises when the participants in a conversation assign different meanings to words. For that reason, it is very important to clarify the meaning of the words we are using before we get too deep into a conversation. We can't have a dialogue if we aren't talking about the same things.

A simple example might be helpful. I often hear groups of educators talk about the importance of student engagement, but when they start to converse, it becomes clear that people define engagement differently. Conversations can spiral downward as people struggle to communicate their ideas to others who misunderstand what's being said. When groups of teachers learn Phil Schlechty's definitions of engagement, for example, their conversation can take off. In *Engaging Students: The Next Level of Working on the Work* (2011), Schlechty distinguishes between (a) authentic engagement, (b) strategic compliance, and (c) retreatism. When a group of educators comes to a shared understanding of the concept of engagement by adopting and understanding Schlechty's terms, they can start to have clear and meaningful dialogue.

Provide Contextual Information. According to the *Oxford English Dictionary* (2012), *context* "is the part or parts preceding or following a passage or word . . . helping to reveal its meaning." Context is additional information that we need to understand what we are talking about or, as the *Oxford English Dictionary* says again, "ambient conditions [or] a set of circumstances" that can help us understand whatever is being communicated.

When we are sharing our thoughts, ideas, and feelings, it is important that we provide a context for what we are sharing. For example, if a teacher is sharing her opinion on what is best for a particular student, she might enhance understanding and the opportunity for dialogue by sharing what she knows about the student or by sharing her own experiences with the options being discussed. When everyone shares the same contextual information, there is a much greater chance that everyone will be able to think together.

> To speak a true word is to transform the world.
>
> **—Paulo Freire**
> (1970, p. 75)

Identify Your False Assumptions About Knowledge. Our false assumptions about what we know (false clarity) or about what our conversation partner knows (the curse of knowledge) can also make it difficult for others to understand what we say.

False Clarity. A major reason we might be unclear is we assume we know more about a topic than we actually do. We think we are being clear, but in truth we either don't have or fail to communicate a depth of knowledge about a topic that we think we have. I have watched many hours of video of coaches describing teaching strategies with great confidence. Unfortunately, despite their confidence, the coaches often describe those strategies superficially, overlooking essential information, or even making statements that are incorrect. Many of those videos, I must admit, were of me.

The Curse of Knowledge. In *Made to Stick: Why Some Ideas Survive and Others Die* (2007), Heath and Heath write about the "curse of knowledge," to which we can fall prey when we learn about something. The authors write that

> once we know something, we find it hard to imagine what it was like not to know it. Our knowledge has cursed us. And it becomes difficult for us to share our knowledge with others, because we can't readily re-create our listeners' state of mind. (p. 20)

Use Stories and Analogies. A final way to be more clear is to use stories and analogies. Stories serve numerous functions: They enable us to shape or structure the general chaos of personal experience; they convey truths too simple or too complex to be stated outright; they help us make sense and meaning of memories and experiences; they prompt us to wrestle with problems and create our own meanings; and they connect us with larger ideas and, perhaps most importantly, to each other.

A story, at its best, provides others with insight into the tacit dimensions of whatever is being discussed. Stories connect us with others who know and have experienced similar events. Good stories remind us of our humanity.

Although stories seem top-down, in reality they are not. A story does begin with one teller, but it only truly becomes

real when listeners hear it and make it something personally meaningful to them. Stories provide clarity, but they
also leave room for others to apply the story to their own
circumstances. A person creates and tells a story, and listeners, in partnership, re-create the story in their minds. As
Richard Stone (1996) commented, listening to a story can be
as creative an act as telling one:

> When you hear my story it is transformed into a tale
> that feels intimately like your own, even palpably
> real and personal, especially if you repeat it to
> another . . . After a few tellings, it no longer matters
> from where these anecdotes and tales originated.
> They take on a life of their own, permeating our
> experiences. (p. 57)

When I was reading to prepare for writing this chapter,
I had a meeting with my colleagues at the Kansas Coaching
Project at the University of Kansas Center for Research on
Learning. In that one-hour meeting, I hastily ignored almost
all of these strategies, which led to a predictable outcome.

We were in the midst of writing a research proposal
to study a statewide instructional coaching project. When
I came to the meeting, I knew we had a lot of things to
accomplish, but I was excited to sit down with the team and
bang out the steps of the project.

We only had an hour, so I asked if it was okay if I laid
out what I saw as our next steps, and after writing up my
ideas on the whiteboard, I asked for everyone's feedback on
how we could break down each component of the proposal.
I was pretty confident we would have an action plan
worked out quickly.

The group, however, wasn't as quick as I had hoped to
list action steps. In fact, they had a lot of questions. How
many coaches would the project serve? How many districts
would be involved? What would we use for our measures?
What are our research questions? These questions could be
worked out eventually, I thought, and I was frustrated that
the team was so slow to break down the details of the plan.

The team also wanted to explore many other finer
points of the project. They wanted to know how often we'd
interact with the district leaders responsible for coaching
the coaches, whether we'd ask them to share video of

themselves coaching, and whether the coaches of coaches would actually be coaches. Then they shared a plan they had put together, which had been emailed to me but I hadn't read, that took the project in another direction.

As we moved along, I got more and more frustrated, and I'm sure my teammates did too. I came to the meeting expecting to engage in dialogue around an exciting project. I was enthusiastic and excited about working with a team of researchers that I truly respected and who have taught me a great deal. By the end, I just wanted the meeting to end. My enthusiasm had turned into compliant resignation. "Why don't you just do what you want, then," I mumbled, and from that point on, I just counted the minutes until the meeting was over.

Looking back, I can see several reasons why this meeting ended up being an anti-dialogical disaster. Certainly a major reason was I had failed to employ many of the strategies described above. We did not have a shared understanding of terms, nor did I give any thought to what my partners might need or feel. What probably would have been most helpful, however, would have been for me to provide contextual information for everyone so that we could indeed engage in dialogue. If we had taken time at the start to confirm everyone's understanding of what we were doing, and if everyone had had time to get a clearer understanding of our project, we might have been able to have a meaningful and helpful dialogue rather than a conversation that, thanks to my impatience, pretty much ended up wasting everyone's time.

INQUIRY

In a dialogue, we must say what we think. However, advocacy without inquiry is anti-dialogical; it leads to a competition of wills where the loudest or most aggressive arguer wins. Dialogue is a partnership activity in which two or more people communicate not to win, but to achieve mutual understanding. As William Isaacs (1999) has written,

> *Advocacy* means speaking what you think, speaking from a point of view. *Inquiry* means looking into what you do not yet understand, or seeking to discover what others see and understand that may be different

from your point of view . . . balancing advocacy and inquiry means stating clearly and confidently what one thinks and why one thinks it, while at the same time being open to being wrong. It means encouraging others to challenge our views, and to explore what might stop them from doing so. (p. 188)

There are several strategies you can employ to encourage inquiry. Among the most powerful are (a) be humble, (b) listen with empathy, (c) open yourself to new ideas, and (d) surface and suspend assumptions.

Be Humble. If I know it all, then I don't need to foster dialogue. Dialogue is a back-and-forth conversation that enables mutual learning, and there is no need for me to learn when I know it all already. This is why Paulo Freire (1970) writes that "dialogue cannot exist without humility" (p. 79). When we embrace Habit 3, Fostering Dialogue, we humbly let go of the notion that there is only one right answer—our answer!—and instead, we choose to see conversation as a testing ground for ideas. A dialogical conversation is something we co-construct with others so everyone in the conversation can learn and grow.

In *Humble Inquiry: The Gentle Art of Asking Instead of Telling* (2013), Edgar Schein writes that humility, "in the most general sense, refers to granting someone else a higher *status* than one claims for oneself" (p. 10). As I see it, in dialogue, humility has a slightly different meaning—it is the willingness to not be right. When we are humble, we clearly communicate our ideas, but we do so provisionally; we embrace the opportunity to find out we are wrong simply because we would rather learn than win.

How then do we become humble? Is it possible to be "really great" at humility? Maybe we need a simple approach to get started. At a minimum, we should strive to keep our self-centeredness and pride under control, like a lion-tamer with a whip keeps the wild beast in its cage. We may never approach Mother Teresa's saintly humility, but we can at least become aware of how our pride and our desire to be right can block our ability to learn.

We can use our imagination to gain perspective on why we should be more humble than we are. First off, when we honestly consider our achievements, we might see that our

> Learning to inquire together about what matters is some of the most significant work I can imagine. Our isolation, our investment in positions and roles, our defense of our own limits, fuel the condition of thinking alone. Dialogue represents a new frontier for human beings—perhaps the true final frontier. In it we can come to know ourselves and our relatedness to the whole of life.
>
> **—William Isaacs**
> (1999, p. 48)

accomplishments are only possible because of the ideas, support, and inspiration we've gotten from others. Also, if we really think about it, we should see that self-centeredness is an unattractive personal trait and our lack of humility can make it difficult for others to respect us. Maybe we can't totally alter our world orientation, but we can learn to put things in perspective. Ironically, when we stop being selfish, good things (more learning and success) will happen.

Emily Manning wrote on her reflection form that when she was working with a first-year teacher, she had to remind herself the new teacher still had knowledge and opinions that she needed to hear. "I need to work on my questioning," Emily wrote, "and really be mindful of the fact that even though she's brand new, she has ideas and opinions to offer. I need to provide more space in our conversation so that we can construct together."

If a major purpose of conversation is learning, the last thing we should be doing is confirming our own conceptions and misconceptions by solely seeking others who see the world the same as us. After all, if we are certain we know it all and don't need to learn, then we are almost certainly wrong.

Listen With Empathy. In Chapter 3, I described why listening with empathy is important and outlined some simple strategies we can all use to become better listeners, so I won't go into great detail here. Listening with empathy makes it possible for us to better advocate for a position, as I explain above, and is even more helpful for promoting inquiry. Indeed, every book or article I read about dialogue identified listening and empathy as essential habits. The back-and-forth sharing of dialogue is only possible when we hear and understand what our conversation partner says.

When Marisol Audia experimented with dialogue for our study of communication skills, she had to learn to take time "to really understand" her conversation partner. "I had to be patient with my conversation partner," she wrote, "and I had to think before responding. I usually have to fill the silence in a conversation since it can make me feel uncomfortable, but when I practiced dialogue, I truly wanted to understand my partner." Marisol also reflected,

"I am not as reactive when I hear something that I don't like. I take time to pause and think before asking and answering questions. I am learning to be quiet."

Daniel Yankelovich in *The Magic of Dialogue* (1999) writes that sometimes we can foster dialogue with what he refers to as "a gesture of empathy" (p. 82), that is, some small action we take or comment we make that communicates that we genuinely understand how a person thinks and feels. Such a gesture could be a helpful action, a truly understanding comment, or an apology. Yankelovich writes:

> The fact that gestures of empathy often come as a surprise tells us something about our society. In our transactions with one another, we are so used to wearing defensive armor that expressions of empathy are unexpected—and disarming. And since disarming is an indispensable prerequisite to dialogue, a gesture of empathy is the quickest and easiest way to start a dialogue. (p. 82)

William Isaacs in *Dialogue and the Art of Thinking Together* (1999) sees listening as essential for learning and dialogue. Isaacs suggests we need to clear our minds and develop "an inner silence" (p. 84) so that we can truly hear others. He also writes that we need to actively listen not just to what people say but "listen for unspoken voices" (p. 298) and try to identify emerging concepts or themes that may not be articulated but which seem to be at play.

Open Yourself to New Ideas. To foster dialogue, you need to be open to what others have to share with you. This means that you value what others have to say or that, as Paulo Freire says, you have faith that others hold within them wisdom, knowledge, ideas, and gifts. As Freire writes (1970), "Faith in [people] is an *a priori* requirement for dialogue; the dialogical [person] believes in other [people] even before . . . meeting them face to face" (p. 79).

To be open is to adopt a learning mindset. Rather than entering into conversations intent to prove that we are right, we enter into conversations with the desire to find out if we are wrong. We can do this by seeking out

One lens that can reduce the temptations to blame and increase respect is to listen to others from the vantage point that says, "This, too, is in me." Whatever the behavior we hear in another, whatever struggle we see in them, we can choose to look for how these same dynamics operate in *ourselves* . . . We may be tempted to say that a given behavior is all "theirs" —I do not have anything like that in me! Maybe so. But the courage to accept it as not only "out there," but also "in here," enables us to engage in the world in a very different way.

—**William Isaacs**
(1999, p. 124)

> Dialogue cannot be carried on in a climate of hopelessness. If the dialoguers expect nothing to come of their efforts, their encounters will be empty, sterile, bureaucratic and tedious.
>
> — **Paulo Freire**
> (1970, p. 80)

what Isaacs calls "disconfirming evidence" (p. 99), information that might help us see that what we are advocating is incorrect.

We also should make it easy for others to tell us what they think even if what they think conflicts with our views. When we are dialogical, we should be nonjudgmental, affirmative, and encouraging. All of the Better Conversations Habits can help to create a setting where real dialogue can occur.

Finally, dialogue can only flourish in situations where there are many possibilities. If we have given up and we are just complaining or blaming, we are not engaging in dialogue. A dialogue is a conversation about a better future. Every dialogue can be a hopeful interaction, proof that we believe a better future is possible. When I listen to you, and you listen to me, there is the hope that we can create something new and better . . . that we can advance thought and create a better tomorrow.

Surface and Suspend Assumptions. One of the most important goals of dialogue is for us to become aware of our assumptions so we can judge them. We can't really be open to learning when we are deeply committed to our own opinions, primarily because we are almost always certain that we are right. Bohm writes:

> Opinions . . . tend to be experienced as "truths," even though they may only be your own assumptions and your own background. You got them from your teacher, your family, or by reading, or in yet some other way. Then for one reason or another you are identified with them, and you defend them. (1996, p. 9)

We defend our assumptions for many reasons. We may want to look strong. Our assumptions might be central to our worldview. Our opinions might be a way of validating how we have lived our lives. Nevertheless, as Bohm has said, "If you are defending a position, you are pushing out what is new" (1996, p. 15).

To be dialogical, as William Isaacs writes, you need to "relax your grip on certainty and listen to the possibilities that result simply from being in a relationship with others—possibilities that might not otherwise have occurred" (1999, p. 19). To balance advocacy with inquiry, we need to suspend our assumptions. This doesn't mean we give up our opinions; it just means we don't make the point of conversation our own point. We accept we might be wrong or right and believe what really matters is learning together. When someone offers a thought that calls into question our opinion, we don't react with anger; we listen, and often we respond by asking a question.

Getting Better at Dialogue

The volunteers on our project who learned about and practiced Habit 3, Fostering Dialogue, reported they became more aware of how they communicated and changed—or at least started to change—the way they communicated after they watched video of themselves practicing dialogue. Emily Manning reported that although she realized she needed to work on questioning, she also noted, "I don't feel as worried about getting every communication right." Jolene Konechne wrote that after watching video of herself in conversation, she realized that she "asked a lot of questions that were not genuine but were actually statements in disguise." Jolene also wrote on her reflection form, "I have become more thoughtful . . . I really think about my questions before each conversation."

The strategies that support Habit 3, Fostering Dialogue, will only become meaningful if people learn them and practice them, especially when they do so while recording themselves in conversation. To help people learn and implement the habit of Fostering Dialogue, three forms are included at the end of this chapter.

The *Looking Back: Fostering Dialogue* form can be used to reflect on a conversation and identify one's assumptions and the assumptions held by others in the conversation.

The *Looking At: Fostering Dialogue* form can be used to analyze whether or not people are engaging in dialogue.

The *Looking Ahead: Fostering Dialogue* form can be used to prepare for a conversation in which one wants to have a dialogue.

I am working on suspending the assumption that I am right, listening authentically to what the other person is saying and really respecting the other person knowing that what they are saying is valuable to them and they deserve to have me hear them . . . I am just really trying to become a better communicator.

—Nicole Patton,
Instructional
Coach, Heartland
AEA, Johnston, Iowa

TO SUM UP

Dialogue is way of communicating where those who are interacting work together to learn from each other and think together. Dialogue is a good idea for practical and moral reasons.

- **Practical:** Dialogue leads to better learning and better outcomes because everyone's brain is involved in the conversation.
- **Moral:** Dialogue is a mutually humanizing form of conversation because everyone is respected and listened to as a fully present human being rather than treated as an object as is the case frequently with top-down communication.

We can foster dialogue by balancing advocacy and inquiry. To foster advocacy we should:

- Consider others' thoughts and feelings
- Clarify the meaning of words and concepts
- Provide contextual information others need so they can understand what we are sharing
- Identify our false assumptions
- Use stories and analogies to help ideas come to life

To foster inquiry we should:

- Be humble
- Listen with empathy
- Open ourselves to new ideas
- Surface and suspend assumptions

GOING DEEPER

My interest in dialogue started with two books, Paulo Freire's *Pedagogy of the Oppressed* (1970) and Peter Senge's *The Fifth Discipline* (1990), both of which are described in other Going Deeper sections in this book. Senge's book introduced me to David Bohm, a scientist who studied quantum theory (whose doctoral advisor was Robert Oppenheimer and who worked with Albert Einstein) and who wrote one of the most influential books on the topic of dialogue. Bohm's *On Dialogue* (first published in 1990) was actually a transcript of a seminar Bohm gave on November 6, 1989. The book is quite short, less than 50 pages in some editions, and reads like an essay more than a book; but, *On Dialogue* is wise, profound, accessible, and required reading for anyone interested in dialogue.

William Isaacs was influenced by both David Bohm and his colleague at MIT, Peter Senge. Isaac's book *Dialogue and the Art of Thinking Together* (1999) is the most thorough treatment of dialogue that I have read. His book is practical, insightful, and inspiring, and Isaac's writing has influenced my thinking on dialogue more than any other.

Daniel Yankelovich's *The Magic of Dialogue: Tranforming Conflict Into Cooperation* (1999) provides practical and inspiring insight into how to define and foster dialogue. His book is a great start for someone not ready to take on Isaacs' 400 pages of thought and practice.

LOOKING BACK:

Fostering Dialogue

//.

Use this form to analyze a conversation where assumptions seemed to get in the way of meaningful dialogue. List the topics that were discussed in the center column. List your assumptions on the right side of the page under the "my assumptions" column. List what you believe your partner's assumptions were on the left side of the page under "others' assumptions."

OTHERS' ASSUMPTIONS	TOPICS DISCUSSED	MY ASSUMPTIONS

Reflections:

LOOKING AT:

Fostering Dialogue (1 of 2)

///.

Complete this form after you have recorded a conversation in which you tried to engage in dialogue. You can complete it while watching or after watching the conversation.

Put a mark on the line to indicate who did most of the thinking in this conversation:

Me   **My Partner**

├──┼──┼──┼──┼──┼──┼──┼──┼──┤
100%   50/50%   100%

Is there anything you can do to ensure both partners contribute equally to the conversation next time?

....

....

Put a mark on the line to indicate what percentage of the time you were talking in this conversation:

Me   **My Partner**

├──┼──┼──┼──┼──┼──┼──┼──┼──┤
100%   50/50%   100%

Is there anything you should do next time to enable your partner to speak more?

....

....

Put a mark on the line that indicates how much of the time you were telling your opinion in the conversation:

                                                    Listening, questioning,
Telling my opinion   **or mutually exploring**

├──┼──┼──┼──┼──┼──┼──┼──┼──┤
100%   50/50%   100%

Is there anything you should do next time to change the way you ask questions?

....

....

....

LOOKING AT:

Fostering Dialogue (2 of 2)

Put a mark on the line that indicates to what extent the outcome of the conversation was one that you proposed, your partner proposed, or was mutually constructed:

Me	Mutual	My Partner
100%	50/50%	100%

Is there anything else you should do to make your next conversation more of a dialogue?

_____

_____

_____

_____

_____

_____

_____

_____

_____

LOOKING AHEAD:

Fostering Dialogue

//

What is your opinion?

_____

_____

_____

What are your conversation partner's needs?

_____

_____

_____

What words do you need to define with your partner?

_____

_____

_____

What contextual information does your partner need to understand what you are talking about?

_____

_____

_____

What stories or analogies can you use to make this conversation clearer?

_____

_____

_____

Are you willing to:

○ not have your opinion accepted?

○ admit you're wrong?

○ listen most of the time—giving everyone equal opportunity to talk?

○ look for disconfirming evidence?

○ suspend your assumptions?

○ identify a devil's advocate?

What else can you do to encourage dialogue?

_____

_____

_____

_____

Available for download at **http://resources.corwin.com/KnightBetterConversations**

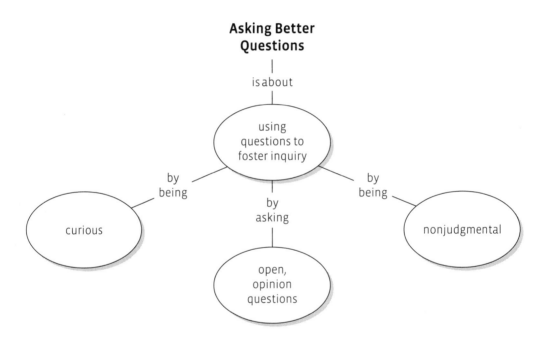

ASKING BETTER QUESTIONS

Why is it so important to learn to ask better questions that help to build positive relationships? Because in an increasingly complex, interdependent, and culturally diverse world, we cannot hope to understand and work with people from different occupational, professional, and national cultures if we do not know how to ask questions and build relationships that are based on mutual respect and the recognition that others know things that we may need to know in order to get a job done.

—Edgar Schein (2013, pp. 1–2)

A good question is like a lever used to pry open the stuck lid on a paint can.

—Frances Peavey, quoted in
Warren Berger (2014, p. 15)

At the Kansas Coaching Project at the University of Kansas Center for Research on Learning, my colleagues and I study instructional coaching by partnering with coaches to learn from them as they try out the practices or processes we develop. Taking this approach to research means we spend a lot of time sitting with coaches, watching videos of conversations, and inventing new ways to make coaching more effective, efficient, and positive.

During one of our first video sessions, we watched several conversations all of us judged to be empty and

> There's never been a better time to be a questioner—because it is so much easier now to begin a journey of inquiry, with so many places you can turn for information, help, ideas, feedback, or even to find possible collaborators who might be interested in the same question.
>
> —Warren Berger
> (2014, p. 28)

low-energy. Coaches and teachers were nice to each other, but didn't seem to talk much about anything that mattered. Then we watched an interview between a research assistant and one of the teachers in our study—a teacher we had watched earlier in the day during one of the flat conversations. Now, when she was asked her opinion, the teacher came alive, and my colleague, Mike Hock, said what we were all thinking: "We need to have our coaching conversations look like that."

The problem with the early coaching conversations was not the coaches; the problem was the way we had asked them to do coaching. Most of the time, coaches were telling teachers what they were doing right and wrong, and none of them were asking powerful questions. The videos taught us better conversations are more about asking than telling, and the energy of human interaction is usually back and forth and not one-directional. We learned that better conversations involve dialogue, and dialogue is made possible by good questions.

Better Questions

Dialogue is not likely going to occur unless we ask effective questions. Good questions open up conversations, generate respect, accelerate learning, and build relationships. Questions are the yang to complete the yin of listening. If we don't ask questions, we won't have the opportunity to listen. If we don't listen, our questions won't serve much purpose. When we see others as equals, we usually give them at least equal time at the center of our conversation, and that requires asking questions that allow our conversation partners to say what they wish. By asking good questions, we demonstrate what Tony Stoltzfus (2008) in *Coaching Questions* calls "conversational generosity." There are three simple and powerful strategies we can use to ask good questions.

Better Questioning Strategies

1. Be curious.

2. Ask open, opinion questions.

3. Be nonjudgmental.

BE CURIOUS

Much has been written about the techniques that good questioners should use. Technique, however, is not as important as the mindset you bring to questioning. As literacy coaching expert Cathy Toll said to me, we shouldn't ask questions to which we think we already know the answer. Rather, we should ask questions because we authentically want to hear what our partner has to say. When we are curious, when we really want to know what others think, we communicate respect for them, and that respect greatly increases the likelihood our partners will speak freely with us.

Curiosity is the embodiment of the principle of reciprocity. When we view conversations as reciprocal, we enter into conversations as learners instead of talkers. When we are curious, we see a conversation as a living interaction that we co-construct with our partner, not a means to tell someone something or an opportunity to control somebody. One way to demonstrate curiosity is by asking for examples. Edgar Schein, in *Humble Inquiry* (2013), writes that "asking for examples is not only one of the most powerful ways of showing curiosity, interest, and concern, but also—and even more important—it clarifies general statements" (p. 33).

William Isaacs (1999) notes many of the questions we ask do not grow out of our curious nature. Isaacs writes,

> [A]n estimated forty percent of all questions that people utter are really statements in disguise. Another forty percent are really judgments in disguise: "Do you really think she deserved that raise?" Only a small percent of "inquires" are genuine questions. (p. 149)

Many questions are used for telling, not answering. Psychologist John Farrell-Higgins, my friend from Topeka, Kansas, identifies four kinds of unhelpful questions: demand questions, set-up questions, stump questions, and angry questions. Demand questions, he says, prompt others to give us an answer we want to hear. For example, a teacher might say after being observed by the principal, "Those kids were really engaged, weren't they?" Set-up questions are used to catch another person in doing something wrong or poorly. Set-up questions can be called "gotcha questions." Thus, a principal might ask, "Did you finish that report on the assessment data?" when she knows the other person hasn't finished the report.

> The missing ingredients in most conversations are curiosity and willingness to ask questions to which we do not already know the answer.
>
> **—Edgar Schein**
> (2013, p. 4)

Stump questions are ones we ask when we know the other person doesn't know an answer, but we do. We ask stump questions so we can demonstrate how smart or knowledgeable we are. For example, we might ask, "Do you know what the effect size is for growth-versus fixed-mindset feedback?" Finally, angry questions are disguised exclamations of negative emotions. A frustrated parent, for example, might ask, "Why don't you give a little thought to what is best for my daughter?"

Unlike these unhelpful questions, when we ask a question out of curiosity, we do so because we genuinely want to hear what the other person has to say. Therefore, when we ask good questions out of curiosity, we are fully present in the conversation. Good questioners give their conversation partners their undivided attention, and they genuinely empathize. Good questioners also let their partners say what they wish by honoring what Susan Scott refers to as the "sweet purity of silence." When you are curious and ask good questions, you communicate respect, build relationships, and you usually learn something important.

ASK OPEN, OPINION QUESTIONS

Much has been written about types and levels of questions, but I believe two basic distinctions are most important: (a) closed versus open questions, and (b) right-or-wrong versus opinion questions.

Closed questions elicit limited responses, and they always ask for answers to which a complete answer can be given. For example, if I ask you the closed question, "What is the new reading program?" you can give me a complete answer simply by naming the program. Closed questions usually invite short, yes or no, factual, or multiple-choice answers.

Open questions elicit unlimited responses and provide the opportunity for an expansive, extended response. For example, if I ask you the open question, "What do you think about the new reading program?" you can theoretically talk as long as you wish during your reply. Open questions usually invite longer, detailed, knowledge, opinion, or feeling answers.

Closed questions can be used effectively to assess whether or not someone has learned something, but they are not especially effective for fostering dialogue. If I want to hear what my conversation partner is thinking or feeling, then open questions are much more effective. However, if I want to confirm my own or someone else's thinking, closed questions work well. For example, Sandra Gearhart found she had to ask closed questions to "clarify my understanding as we determined levels for progress monitoring."

Right-or-wrong questions, as the name implies, are questions for which there are correct or incorrect answers. On the other hand, opinion questions are questions to which there are no specific correct answers since they prompt people to give their own opinion. The question, "Who is the president?" is both a closed and a right-or-wrong question because there is only one correct answer to it. Similarly, our example of an open question, "What do you think about the president?" is also an example of an opinion question. I may not agree with your answer, but when you tell me what you think, your answer is your opinion, not an attempt to give a correct reply.

Right-or-wrong questions, like closed questions, can be used effectively to confirm understanding, but they are rarely successful during open conversations. When asked right-or-wrong questions, people are often hesitant to respond for fear of being wrong. However, when asked opinion questions, they are much more forthcoming.

In *Make Just One Change: Teach Students to Ask Their Own Questions* (2011), Dan Rothstein and Luz Santana write that "open-ended questions start with *Why* and *How?* Close-ended questions start with *Is? Do?* and *Can?* [and] words that could be used for both types of questions [include] *What?*, *Who?*, *Where?*, and *When?*" (p. 81).

These distinctions between open and closed questions and right-or-wrong and opinion questions may seem obvious, but in my experience, the most common mistake people make during questioning is to use closed or right-or-wrong questions as vehicles for conversation. When a workshop leader or a meeting facilitator asks a question that falls dead, the reason is almost always that the question was not an opinion question.

> I've been more conscious of being a listener, not interrupting, and asking fat, open-ended questions that really encourage elaborate responses. I find myself really listening for things I can follow up on with questions that will get the speaker to give more information and get the other person to be more passionate about the topic of the dialogue.
>
> **—Molly Edelen,** Special Education Teacher, Mathias, West Virginia, describing what she learned about questioning while talking with her daughter about the Disney Channel

> This work, asking questions, is hard work. I've had to do more thinking than I've ever done…Can we do this again tomorrow?
>
> **—An adult education student,** quoted in Rothstein & Santana (2011, p. 7)

Why . . .

1. Why are students dropping out?

2. Why does student engagement decrease the longer students are in school?

3. Why aren't students motivated to learn?

4. Why don't students feel psychologically safe?

5. Why are teacher evaluations usually done in the last months of school?

What if . . .

6. What if students had more voice in what they are learning?

7. What if I change my questions from closed to open questions?

8. What if our school commits to implementing the Better Conversations Beliefs and Habits across the school to create a psychologically safe environment for students and teachers?

9. What if teachers evaluate themselves using video at several points during the year?

How . . .

10. How can I teach to the standards while still giving students an authentic voice?

11. How can I use video to monitor my questions?

12. How often and in what kind of groups should we meet to study the Better Conversations Beliefs and Habits?

13. How can we support teachers so their own evaluations of their teaching are reliable and based on objective standards of teaching excellence?

In his book *A More Beautiful Question: The Power of Inquiry to Spark Breakthrough Ideas* (2014), Warren Berger argues that questioning is an essential habit for people to unlock creativity and purpose in their daily lives and for businesses to unlock growth and innovation. Berger supports his claim by quoting Stuart Firestein:

> One good question can give rise to several layers of answers, can inspire decades-long searches for solutions, can generate whole new fields of inquiry, and can prompt changes in entrenched thinking . . . Answers, on the other hand, often end the process. (p. 16)

Berger writes that "open questions . . . tend to encourage creative thinking more than closed yes-or-no questions" (p. 18), and based on his research, he suggests three essential questions: "Why, What If, and How." Berger shows that these three questions stand at the heart of many game-changing innovations, including the invention of the microwave oven, Gatorade, Netflix, windshield wipers, the World Wide Web, and many other innovations.

The "Why, What If, and How" questions could be used in schools. For example, students engaged in project-based authentic learning could structure their projects around the questions. Instructional coaches could use the questions to give focus to coaching interactions with teachers. In the box on page 96, I suggest how the questions might be used to address issues in schools.

BE NONJUDGMENTAL

If we want people to engage in a conversation around questions, we need to ensure that they feel psychologically safe. This means that we do not judge them when they answer. This, of course, is simply living out the Better Conversations Belief that I don't judge my conversation partners.

There are two simple things you can do to not be judgmental when asking questions. First, after you ask a question, you need to listen without assumptions and without prejudging your conversation partner. If you jump to conclusions about what your partner says, chances are he or she will notice and then be less open.

Second, to remain nonjudgmental when you ask questions, let go of the desire to give advice. For some reason most of us have an almost uncontrollable desire to tell others how they should go about their business. However, in almost all cases, our partners don't want advice unless they explicitly ask for it. What people want is someone who listens, values their ideas, and is empathetic and nonjudgmental.

When we ask better questions, we do not use questions to make a statement or direct the conversation to the destination we have chosen. We ask the question because we are genuinely interested. Edgar Schein refers to this dialogical approach as humble inquiry. "Humble inquiry," Schein writes, "is the skill and art of drawing someone out, of asking questions to which you do not already know the answer, of building a relationship based on curiosity and interest in people" (2013, p. 21).

Getting Better at Questioning

When Susan Hope experimented with the habit of better questions for our global communication study, she found that focusing on the three simple questioning strategies (be curious, ask open, opinion questions, and be nonjudgmental) made it easier for her to improve. "Sometimes as a coach, I feel like I have so much thinking going on in my head that I miss out on the conversation. I especially liked the three simple steps and being able to focus on the parts I needed."

The volunteers who studied their questioning found that video helped them better understand the kind of questions and how they asked questions. Susan Hope wrote, "While I was pleased with my actual questions, I heard myself making judgments about their ideas, so that will be something I need to work on." Joellen Killion's experiences also suggest people should monitor their habits carefully as they experiment. Joellen found when she was doing the research project, she "asked more questions rather than fewer," and she wrote, "I feel if I had just listened, I would have gotten everything the person wanted to say without working so hard." When we implement the Better Conversations Habits, we need to monitor how well the habits fit with our personality and learning approach and modify their use as necessary.

To help people learn and implement the habit of better questions, three forms are included at the end of this chapter.

The *Looking Back: Asking Better Questions* form can be used by people to analyze whether their questions are open or closed, right or wrong, or opinion.

The *Looking At: Asking Better Questions* form can be used by people to record the effective and ineffective questions they hear in conversations each day.

The *Looking Ahead: Asking Better Questions* form lists many questions that have been suggested by questioning experts so people can plan to ask better questions in the future.

Being nonjudgmental was not difficult for me. I understand the importance of teachers trusting me, and feeling they can be open, and express their opinions.

—Sandra Gearhart,
Instructional
Support Coach,
St. Charles, Illinois

TO SUM UP

When we adopt Habit 4, Asking Better Questions, we communicate respect for others because (a) we don't know the answer to our questions, and (b) we really want to hear what others have to say.

Three strategies are a part of Habit 4, Asking Better Questions—(a) be curious, (b) ask open, opinion questions, and (c) be nonjudgmental.

- **Be curious:** We can demonstrate curiosity by only asking questions we don't know the answer to and by asking for examples. We should avoid asking the unhelpful questions identified by John Farrell-Higgins—demand, set-up, stump, or angry questions—and avoid asking questions that are really statements in disguise.
- **Ask open, opinion questions:** To promote inquiry and dialogue, we should ask open questions (which elicit unlimited responses and provide the opportunity for expansive, extended responses) and opinion questions (which have no specific, correct answer).
- **Be nonjudgmental:** We can ensure people feel psychologically safe by being certain not to judge them when they answer questions.

Warren Berger's (2014) *why, what if, how* questioning framework can be applied in many settings, including personal planning, coaching, and teaching.

GOING DEEPER

Edgar Schein's *Humble Inquiry: The Gentle Art of Asking Instead of Telling* (2013) is my favorite book about questioning. Schein simply explains why we should listen with respect and ask with humility if we want to lead effectively—or for that matter, if we want to experience healthy relationships. Schein is especially helpful at clarifying how status and questioning are interwoven.

Dan Rothstein and Luz Santana's *Make Just One Change: Teach Students to Ask Their Own Questions* (2011) describes an elegant and powerful process for increasing student engagement and learning by giving them the opportunity to create, analyze, and explore their own questions about learning. Rothstein and Santana's book is persuasive, and I think anyone interested in increasing student engagement or learning should consider reading it and experimenting with their ideas. The book also contains excellent definitions of different types of questions.

Warren Berger's *A More Beautiful Question: The Power of Inquiry to Spark Breakthrough Ideas* (2014) is a passionate argument for the importance of questioning. Berger makes the case that questioning should be at the heart of K–12 education, innovation in organizations, and personal planning. I especially found Berger's anecdotes to be interesting. For example, he explains that Bette Nesmith Graham invented what eventually became Whiteout after asking the question, "What if we could paint over our mistakes?" Graham eventually sold her invention for approximately $50,000,000.00 and gave half of it to her son Michael Nesmith, the song writer, executive producer, and former lead guitarist of The Monkees.

LOOKING BACK:

Asking Better Questions

Audio or video record a conversation. The conversation could be at work, home, or in the community, but pick an important one (for example, a goal-setting conversation, if you are a coach). Make sure your conversation partner is OK with your recording it. Afterward, listen to your conversation and code your questions.

QUESTION	OPEN	CLOSED	OPINION	RIGHT/WRONG
	○	○	○	○
	○	○	○	○
	○	○	○	○
	○	○	○	○
	○	○	○	○
	○	○	○	○
	○	○	○	○
	○	○	○	○
	○	○	○	○
	○	○	○	○
	○	○	○	○
	○	○	○	○
	○	○	○	○
	○	○	○	○
	○	○	○	○
	○	○	○	○
	○	○	○	○
	○	○	○	○
	○	○	○	○

LOOKING AT:

Asking Better Questions

Use this area to record effective questions you hear during day-to-day conversation. Effective questions usually provoke thought, dialogue, or foster better conversations in other ways. Effective questions are often open and opinion questions.

Use this area to record ineffective questions you hear during day-to-day conversation. Ineffective questions often have obvious answers, fail to provoke thought, and usually do not foster better conversations. Ineffective questions are often closed, right/wrong questions.

LOOKING AHEAD:

Asking Better Questions

Identify a future conversation where you will need to ask effective questions. Review the list of questions below to identify questions you might use to foster dialogue and share understanding. Put a checkmark beside any questions you might use in the identified conversation.

QUESTION

○ Given the time we have today, what is the most important thing you and I should be talking about? (Susan Scott)

○ What if nothing changes? So what? What are the implications for you and your students? (Susan Scott)

○ What is the ideal outcome? (Susan Scott)

○ What can we do to resolve this issue? (Susan Scott)

○ Tell me about what you felt.

○ Tell me a little about this...

○ What leads you to believe....?

○ What went well? What surprised you? What did you learn? What will you do differently next time?

○ What do you think about....?

○ On a scale of 1-10, how close are you to your ideal classroom? (Steve Barkley)

○ What are you seeing that shows that the strategy is successful? (Steve Barkley)

○ What impact would _____ have? (Steve Barkley)

○ When have you seen _____? (Steve Barkley)

○ What do you think the _____ suggests?

○ What are some other ways we can look at that?

○ What are we uncertain about?

○ What is your hope for _____?

○ What if nothing happens?

Available for download at **http://resources.corwin.com/KnightBetterConversations**

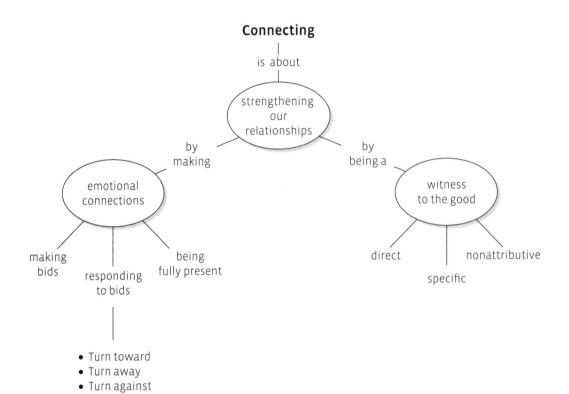

CONNECTING

Connection is why we're here. We are hardwired to connect with others, it's what gives purpose and meaning to our lives, and without it, there is suffering.

—Brené Brown (2012, p. 8)

I need to slow down and take the time to care. I cannot continue to walk past people and throw out a random "How are you?" and keep walking. I can't be so work-minded that I miss out on knowing people better. The people who are walking down the hallway all have things going well in their live and things that are consuming their thoughts. I need to get to know those people better.

—Rhonda Fode,
Instructional Coach, Detroit Lakes
School District, Detroit Lakes, Minnesota

My fitness coach, Lisa, is one of the most positive people I know. Whenever I meet with her, she has stories to tell me about the inspiring books she's reading, her warm-hearted miraculous interactions with other people, and the ideas she has about how we should go about getting better. She is encouraging and positive every time I see her. When I told her I was writing a book about communication, she quickly volunteered to try out the Better Conversation process.

I sent Lisa an early draft of this chapter on emotional connection, and she told me she would apply the ideas right away. Then a few days later, she texted me. "This emotional connection stuff is really hard," she wrote.

Lisa and I met at the gym soon after that. She told me that she had texted her adult daughter. Lisa had gone through a difficult divorce, and her daughter had stopped communicating with her. After reading an early draft of this chapter, Lisa texted her daughter and asked her if she would consider reconnecting. Lisa heard nothing back. In typical Lisa fashion, she had applied the ideas from the book to the part of her life where they could have the biggest impact, but also where there was the biggest risk. Few things are more difficult than feeling separated from your children.

On my next trip to the gym, however, I learned that everything had changed. With tears in her eyes, Lisa told me her daughter had written back. She wanted to reconnect. She was coming to visit Lisa for a weekend, and their relationship had turned a gigantic corner. One text message won't heal every old wound, and no doubt Lisa and her daughter had difficult conversations as they overcame their years of separation, but they would not be reconnecting if Lisa hadn't reached out. By taking the initiative to make a connection, Lisa started to heal one of the most important relationships in her life.

My guess is that many of us have relationships like Lisa's with her daughter, relationships where communication may not have broken down completely, but where we do not feel as connected as we would like to. Maybe we feel a lack of connection with friends, family, coworkers, or people in our community. If we understand how our actions can nurture or damage emotional connection, we can start to have better conversations.

Making Emotional Connections

One of the world's leading experts on relationships, John Gottman, sees emotional connection as the primary goal of relating to others. Gottman and Joan DeClaire (2001) put it this way:

[W]hether people are struggling to save a marriage, to cooperate in a family crisis, or to build rapport with a difficult boss, they usually have one thing in common: They need to share emotional information that can help them feel connected. (p. 3)

Gottman and DeClaire's (2001) research provides us with a simple strategy for observing behavior and coaching ourselves on how well we build up or tear down our emotional connection with others. According to Gottman and DeClaire, emotional connection is fueled or frustrated by how we reach out to connect (*bids*) and how we respond (turning toward, turning away, turning against) to others' bids. I've described each of these responses below.

Bids. Gottman and DeClaire (2001) describe the bid as "the fundamental unit of emotional communication . . . A bid can be a question, gesture, a look, a touch—any single expression that says 'I want to feel connected to you'" (p. 4). Participants in our study were quick to identify bids they and others made. Some bids they observed were questions such as asking a new teacher about her first year, or asking a grandmother to talk about her granddaughter. Some were actions such as offering to drive someone to a doctor's appointment when there was a chance of bad news, or helping a senior citizen load peat moss into her car. The bids volunteers described also included statements such as telling a teenager that his driving is improving or complimenting a waiter for great service in restaurants. Bids, as Laura Browder wrote on her reflection form, could include "smiles, head nods, verbal greetings, physical touch (hugs, handshakes, hand on shoulders, etc.), compliments, text messages and so forth."

Turning Toward. Gottman and DeClaire (2001) write that we "turn toward" someone who offers us an emotional bid when we respond positively toward that invitation. If we are invited out to dinner, we say yes, or we acknowledge the thoughtfulness of the invitation. If someone smiles, we smile back. Rhonda Fode, as part of her personal experiment with emotional connection, spent 30 minutes in a coffee shop watching people interact to watch for examples of people building emotional connections. On her reflection form, she wrote that "as soon as the bid became personal, people turned toward the bid. They moved closer, faced each other, and smiled. Their faces opened and they spoke louder. There was an ongoing conversation where connections were made."

> Our findings about the bidding process give me a tremendous amount of hope. They tell me that people who consistently bid and respond to bids in positive ways have an astounding chance for success in their relationships.
>
> **—John Gottman and Joan DeClaire**
> (2001, p. 6)

When someone turns toward our bid, we feel seen, validated, and happy. Educational consultant Lisa Sligh experienced that positive emotion when she and a parent of one of her students texted back and forth. "I wrote to validate her concerns and simply mention the strengths of her child and how he would shine," Lisa wrote. When the parent wrote to Lisa saying, "you are always so awesome and positive," Lisa wrote, "I did a happy dance."

Turning Away. When we turn away from a bid, we fail to respond to the bid for emotional connection. Often, this means we don't even notice that someone else has made a bid for connection. Gottman and DeClaire (2001) observe that turning away "is rarely malicious or mean-spirited. More often we're simply unaware of or insensitive to others' bids for our attention" (p. 5). Volunteers in our study shared many examples of how they turned away from others' bids for connection because they were distracted by whatever else they were doing. Often the distractions involved technology, work, or simply the thoughts going through their minds. Laura Browder wrote on her reflection sheet, "when I did miss a bid, it was usually because I was busy in my head formulating my next response. When I watched our conversation on video, I saw that I actually missed both the bid and what she was saying."

Turning away, according to Gottman and DeClaire (2001), can be devastating:

> When somebody turns away from a bid, the bidder loses confidence and self-esteem . . . people almost seem to "crumple" when their partners turn away. The bidders don't get puffed up with anger; they don't get indignant; they just seem to fold in on themselves. On video we can see their shoulders sag slightly as if they've been deflated. They feel defeated. They give up. (p. 47)

Turning Against. Gottman and DeClaire (2001) explain that when people turn against bids, they react in argumentative or hostile ways. For example, if a coach offers to provide a model lesson for a teacher, a teacher who turns against might reply by saying, "What in the world would I learn from you?" Instructional coach Carol Walker described a conversation she was observing where teachers and a principal were interrupted by someone who wanted to join in their conversation, but who wasn't welcome. "The teachers," Carol wrote, "gave one another 'the look' that said, 'Be careful, this person is nosey again. You know what a gossip she is.' And the principal made it clear with tone and body language that she was intruding."

Gottman and DeClaire's (2001) research on emotional connection has been especially helpful for my colleagues and me at the Kansas Coaching Project because it has given us a vocabulary for understanding emotional connection. The coaches I work with talk about how they make and respond to bids for connection. And when they study their own conversation, the video does not lie. Coaches who watch video recordings of their coaching conversations discover that they frequently miss opportunities for turning toward bids.

BUILDING EMOTIONAL CONNECTIONS

We can deepen our connections with others by learning to practice two strategies. First we need to *be fully present* when we are with others, and become sensitive to the ways in which people extend emotional bids for connection and how we respond to those bids. We also need to *be persistent*, making bids and continuing to attempt to connect even when others do not, at first, turn toward those bids.

Be Fully Present. The volunteers who took on the emotional connection challenge observed how they and others built or damaged relationships by encouraging or blocking emotional connection. Everyone reported that they gained much deeper insight into how important emotional connection is for relationships. The bids people observed were not always profound life-changing events, although some were. They often were simple moments experienced in the day-to-day routines of life. One research participant, for example, shared a simple example of a bid. When she was out for dinner with friends, they discovered that it was their server's birthday. When her table sang "Happy Birthday" to their server, which was a simple, fun bid, the server, she wrote, "beamed and told the group that she had recently gotten a divorce, and this was her first post-divorce

---

Connect

A Bid: Can be a question, a gesture, a look, a touch—any single expression that says "I want to be connected to you." (Gottman & DeClaire, p. 4)

Turning Toward: Means to react in a positive ways to another's bids for emotional connection. (p. 16)

Turning Away: This pattern of relating generally involves ignoring another's bid, or acting preoccupied. (p. 17)

Turning Against: People who turn against one another's bids for connection might be described as belligerent or argumentative. For example, if a man fantasized about owning a passing sports car, his friend might reply, "On your salary? Dream on!" (p. 17)

I do believe that the practices I am focused on at this point made the difference with me and my attitude the last month of school. I hope that the change in my thinking may be of a positive influence for the women in our department with whom I am close. I am convinced that the challenges that began this spring will resurrect in the fall. And, I think I will be better equipped to handle these issues if I can keep practicing these skills.

—Research volunteer

birthday." It was a small gesture, but everyone felt better for having the experience. Often it is the smallest actions that have the biggest impact.

All of the volunteers on this study described the life-enriching power of emotional connection, and yet most people reported that they learned, through our project, that they missed far too many opportunities to connect. Stephanie Barnhill's comments were typical. She wrote "that she learned that she has to stop getting so wrapped up in coaching that she forgets to relate to the human side of people." Almost every volunteer wrote describing moments when they missed opportunities to connect because they were so focused on work, or a task, or the busyness of their life, or just the many ideas swirling in their minds. Most volunteers described how their technology interfered with connection. When people pull out their phones, they shut down connections.

Since relationships are vital at work, and even more important in our personal life, we need a strategy to act in ways that help us help relationships flourish: that strategy is to be fully present. Carolyn Matteson wrote that learning to be fully present and to pay attention to bids and not turn away was a very important lesson. "If I am missing occasions when someone is bidding for my attention or if I am bidding for someone else's attention and don't even recognize it, I am missing something important. That is something I need to keep coaching myself about."

We will be more effective at building emotional connections if we notice when other people make bids to connect with us. As Gottman and DeClaire (2001) write, "if you don't pay attention, you don't connect" (p. 66). To be fully present, of course, is an essential practice for many of the habits described in this book, especially demonstrating empathy and listening. We can't listen if we don't hear, we can't demonstrate empathy if we aren't aware of our conversation partner, and we can't connect unless we pay attention and watch for opportunities to connect.

When one study participant paid attention to how she connected with others, she realized, she said, "that it sounded easier than it was." She learned that she "had to be aware and not just go through the motions." When we watch, listen, and demonstrate empathy, we will have more opportunities to connect. And more connection should mean we experience much healthier relationships, even much more love.

Being fully present is also a way to show respect for others. Fewer things are more disrespectful than simply ignoring others. And yet, too often we allow ourselves to be distracted by Facebook when a fully alive, warm-hearted human being stands beside us. We fill out some trivial, online personality quiz when we could have experienced a better conversation.

William Isaacs (1999) writes that being fully present, that is, really seeing others, is a way we respect and legitimize others.

> In Zulu, a South African language, the word *Sawu bona* is spoken when people greet one another and when they depart. It means "I see you." To the Zulus, being seen has more meaning than in Western cultures. It means that the person is in some real way brought more fully into existence by virtue of the fact that they are seen. As in most indigenous cultures, the memory of a sense of participation in nature has not been completely lost. To say "I see you" is to sustain you in this world. (p. 111)

One way to learn to be fully present is to simply watch other people to get a deeper understanding of how people connect or fail to connect. Gottman and DeClaire's (2001) work helps us name and see phenomena that we wouldn't see if we didn't have their words. The concepts of bids, turning toward, turning away, and turning against help us see people living out those concepts all the time right in front of us.

When we watch how people bid and respond to bids, we start to see how simple actions can open up or shut down emotional connection. The nonverbal and verbal ways in which people interact can be revealing. When we observe others, we should watch to see whether we see someone light up when a friend makes a bid. Do we see a flash of sadness when someone turns away? There is much to be learned by setting aside time to simply pay attention to people around you and note how they interact.

Complex, fulfilling relationships don't suddenly appear in our lives fully formed. Rather, they develop one encounter at a time.

—**John Gottman and Joan DeClaire**
(2001, p. 6)

If you can see past a person's anger, sadness, or fear to recognize the hidden need, you open up new possibilities for relation. You're able to see your coworker's sullen silence as a bid for inclusion in decisions that affect his job, for example. Or you can recognize that your sister's agitation says she's feeling alienated from the family. You can even see the bid in your three-year-old's temper tantrum: He not only wants the toy you can't buy for him, he wants your comfort in a frustrating situation, as well.

—John Gottman and
Joan DeClaire
(2001, p. 36)

Bids and responses happen anywhere people get together, in homes, schools, shopping malls, parks, coffee shops, and places of worship. One way to deepen our understanding of the dynamics of emotional connection is to set aside a short period of time to people watch. You might do this by going to your local coffee shop, grabbing your favorite beverage, and using the *Looking At* form at the end of this chapter to focus your perceptions.

Be Persistent. To build connection, of course, we don't just respond to bids, but we reach out to make connections with others. This can be done in many different ways. We can make a point of showing interest in people's lives and families. We can find out what our conversation partners are interested in and ask them about their interests. We can write thank-you notes and place them in people's mailboxes.

If we find innovative ways to make bids for connection, and if we are mindful of how bids shape the emotional landscape of our schools, homes, and communities, we should find many opportunities to turn toward bids from others. To do this, we need to take the time to listen, observe, and interact. Taking the time to connect with others is just as important as taking the time to observe in the classroom. People long for connection, and that takes time. Emotionally intelligent leaders are constantly watching for opportunities to respond positively to others' bids for connection. Sometimes this means we have to keep trying even when others turn away or against.

One participant learned about the importance of being persistent when he volunteered for our study. He wrote on his reflection form that when he studied his communication style, he discovered that he had to persevere with his attempts to connect even when others didn't return his bids for connection. After he completed the self-coaching project, he wrote, "I am more apt to try to go the extra mile, to take the extra step to do something nice, to help out, or to try to help someone to feel good. It doesn't always work in return, I guess since there are some unpleasant people out there. But it is worth the effort."

Volunteers in our study found that learning to make and respond to bids can have a huge impact on relationships, but making and responding to bids won't make a difference if our external behavior is not reinforced by internal integrity. Understanding Gottman and DeClaire's vocabulary is no replacement for respect, empathy, care, honesty, and affection. We can't make a bunch of bids and figure everything will be all right. We need to be honest, for example, or our dishonesty will eventually be found out and expose our bids as hollow and inauthentic. For this reason, the Better Conversations Beliefs are especially important. When we see others as equals, and we want to hear what they have to say, and we expect conversation to be life-giving, our bids for connection will resonate and build relationships. If our bids are a cover for dishonesty, or self-centeredness, or our belief that it is OK to manipulate others, our bids will eventually be exposed as fake. Superficial or inauthentic bids for connection might actually damage a relationship.

INCREASING EMOTIONAL CONNECTION

We can improve our connection with others by being fully present and by being persistent, but we have to learn and internalize these habits. We can do that, as many of the volunteers on our study did, by video recording a conversation with someone who doesn't object to the presence of the camera (preferably someone with whom we interact frequently) and then reviewing the form with the *Looking Back* form in hand. You can use the form to identify times when you or your conversation partner made bids and then to observe how each of you responded to bids. This activity in particular helps us to become more mindful of how we respond to our partner's bids for connection. We become more sensitive to the richness of human interaction.

Ben Collins is an assistant principal in Maine West High School in Des Plaines, Illinois, just north of Chicago. He volunteered to work on Habit 5, Making Emotional Connections, and he carefully paid attention to how people built and damaged personal connections. For our study, Ben kept a running log of his bids for connection, observed other people's bids for connection, and video recorded himself in conversation to see how he went about connecting with others.

I think the real challenge in making emotional bids to increase personal connection is to not take it personally when a bid is responded to with a turn away or against. It is quite an ironic process—making attempts to build personal connections and then not taking the response personally! However, it really has so much more to do with my conversation partners and less about me. Often their response is more an indication of where they stand emotionally within themselves and not so much about me. Resilience is required then to keep making those emotional bids for personal connection even when the responses are not what you hoped for.

—**Andrea Bromell,**
Title I Resource Teacher, Boinbridge Elementary School, Cecil County, Maryland

I used to teach high school music and I have some friends who have perfect pitch, but when they sit and listen to music they have a hard time listening to something that is out of tune. Studying how to build emotional connection for me is really just a tuning experience for your emotions and your relationships. When you start to tune into your own habits, you see things differently and it's really important. Sometimes you don't like what you see. But you need to stay positive with everybody that you are working with because some people really need that, even if they aren't especially in tune with their emotions.

—Ben Collins,
Assistant Principal,
Des Plaines, Illinois

When I interviewed Ben, after I read his reflection forms, he told me what he learned from the project. "I think you are in the worst position possible to make any judgments about yourself," Ben said, "until you see it from a different perspective." Ben found it "really interesting" to watch how people negotiated emotional connection. "I noticed that there are some people who are really good at building connections naturally, and some people who could really work on this. I put myself in the category of really needing to work on it," Ben said.

What Ben found when he watched others was that Gottman's concepts gave him "a different lens for viewing people. Before I would think," Ben said, "'Oh this person is really kind.' Now I am seeing that they are doing certain little miniscule things to build connections even if they are doing them subconsciously."

Ben saw that others "acknowledged everything more quickly" than he did, and when he tried to improve, Ben "saw a really big impact right away." On his reflection form Ben wrote, "Today, I have a type of radar out for those times where I can share a connection with someone, and it has made me much more present in my professional and personal life. Schools can be such fast-paced environments that we forget about some of those things. I think this helps you really focus on encouraging others. Now," Ben said, "I make a conscious effort to make a connection every time. If I can increase the intentional bids in my life, I think I can improve my relationships and be a more effective partner in whatever I'm doing. I'd like to be an aggressive bidder and seek out more ways to be kind."

GETTING BETTER AT CONNECTING

The volunteers in our study, like Ben Collins, found great value in observing and reflecting on how they communicate with others. Carolyn Matteson, for example, wrote the following on her reflection form:

[My] awareness is much more acute. Sometime it's almost like those "out of body" experiences you hear about. I'm hovering somewhere above or outside the interaction, watching and assessing and coaching myself. In fact, that sense of watching and coaching myself is so much more common these days that it doesn't make me self-conscious about the choices I am making as a result—to smile, to ask a related question, to offer a word of encouragement or appreciation for something my conversation partner has said or done.

Several forms are included at the end of the chapter to help you get better at connecting.

Use the *Looking Back: Making Emotional Connections* form to carefully analyze a video-recorded conversation. The form simply guides you to consider what your conversation partner did to build emotional connection.

Use the *Looking At: Making Emotional Connections (1 of 2)* form to focus your observations as you watch people around you negotiate emotional connections. Many of the volunteers on our project found this activity, made possible by this form, to be very helpful.

Use the *Looking At: Making Emotional Connections (2 of 2)* form to keep a record of the bids you make throughout the day. The purpose of the form is to increase the number of bids for emotional connection you make every day. You shouldn't spend more than a few seconds filling out the form, and you won't be able to record all interactions, but keeping the form at hand and in mind, you can start to initiate more emotional connections. This is the form Ben Collins used to get a deeper understanding of the different kinds of bids he made each day.

Use the *Looking Ahead: Making Emotional Connections* form to plan to make and respond to more bids. You can use this form to set up a plan to make an emotional connection with someone. This is the form Lisa, whose story I included at the beginning of this chapter, used to connect with her daughter. The form guides you through a few simple steps you can take to start connecting more intentionally with someone.

Being a Witness to the Good

One of the simplest and most powerful ways to build emotional connections is by sharing positive information with others. When people share positive information, they validate, encourage, and sometimes inspire others. When I work with coaches, we often refer to the act of watching for and commenting on the positive things others do as "being a witness to the good." As business guru Tom Peters has commented, "The simple act of paying positive attention to people has a great deal to do with productivity."

When Bonnie Tomberlin was experimenting with Habit 6, Being a Witness to the Good, for our global study of communications, she found herself in a difficult position. As a coach of coaches and a director for a statewide project in Kentucky, one of Bonnie's responsibilities was to conduct implementation checks, which required her to meet with co-teaching teams to discuss how well they were doing.

While she was studying how to be a witness to the good, Bonnie had to meet with a team with whom she had not had a very good experience during the previous year. "This was the second implementation check for me to complete," Bonnie wrote. "The initial check was extremely difficult as there was a toxic culture issue in the building that had tainted the team. The first check was exactly a year earlier, and it was hard. I left very discouraged about the team's future." Bonnie was not looking forward to this second implementation check, and she wrote, "I think they were dreading my visit as much as I was."

Bonnie went to the school determined to be a witness to the good. She was intent to see and communicate "specific evidence that supported the general praise she wanted to give. Fortunately," Bonnie wrote, "a positive change in the building culture had broken through to the team's classroom," and Bonnie was able to spend "a good portion of our feedback time discussing how well the team had embraced the changes and how it had had a positive impact on students."

Bonnie took notes so that she could be very specific about what went well, and when everyone met, she told the team what she saw. "As I listened to the conversation at your round table, I heard thought-provoking questions and varied answers. I saw teammates struggling with new concepts, but they were not pushing back, they were struggling to learn. I noticed respect and authentic engagement during your team meeting." When the team heard her comments, Bonnie wrote, they were "surprised, grateful, and teary-eyed."

Bonnie herself was surprised that she felt "as humbled and moved by their responses." "Successes like these," Bonnie wrote, "are measured in smiles, hugs, and tears."

When we are a witness to the good, others may feel encouraged, validated, boosted, and sometimes inspired. Martin Seligman identifies positive emotion as one of five critical factors for emotional well-being and, as he explains, positive emotion almost always occurs in relationships. In his landmark book *Flourish: A Visionary New Understanding of Happiness and Well-Being* (2011), he writes the following:

> Very little that is positive is solitary. When was the last time you laughed uproariously? The last time you felt indescribable joy? The last time you sensed profound meaning and purpose? The last time you felt enormously proud of an accomplishment? Even without knowing the particulars of these high points in your life, I know their form: all of them took place around other people. (p. 20)

People who are highly sensitive to the positive things that others do can provide a great service to the educators in a school. Too often, the challenges of being an educator and the emotional exhaustion that comes with trying to reach every child every day make it difficult for teachers to fully comprehend the good they are doing. Furthermore, the conversations in schools sometimes have a tendency to turn negative, perhaps as a defense mechanism for teachers who are frustrated that they cannot reach more students. Kegan and Lahey (2001), who have studied conversations in numerous organizations, report that people frequently undercommunicate the positive aspects of their work:

> Nearly every organization or work team we've spent time with . . . astonishingly undercommunicates the genuinely positive, appreciative, and admiring experiences of its members. This . . . is a terrible deprivation of the vitality of the work setting. (pp. 91–92)

Thus, a very valuable service we can provide is to communicate the "genuinely positive, appreciative, and admiring experiences" of the people we see. Indeed, perhaps we should consider it one of our goals to change

> Being a witness to the good has served as a great reminder to expect and believe the best of those I am coaching.
>
> **—Bonnie Tomberlin,**
> Consultant,
> Kentucky
> Department of
> Education, Frankfort,
> Kentucky

We do not believe in ourselves until someone reveals that deep inside us is something valuable, worth listening to, worthy of our trust, sacred to our touch. Once we believe in ourselves we can risk curiosity, wonder, spontaneous delight, or any experience that reveals the human spirit.

—**Author unknown**

the kind of conversations that take place around us by being a witness to the good.

WHY IT IS DIFFICULT TO BE A WITNESS TO THE GOOD

Top-Down and Bottom-Up Attention. Winifred Gallagher, in *Rapt: Attention and the Focused Life* (2009), helped me understand why it is difficult—almost unnatural—to be a witness to the good. Gallagher describes two types of attention that we may bring to any experience. *Bottom-up attention* is the attention we use when we notice something we can't help noticing. For example, if the bell goes off at the end of a period in school, the sound will get everyone's attention—in fact, the sound is designed to do just that. Our bottom-up attention helps us notice pleasant things like the scent of fresh-baked cookies or unpleasant sounds like a crying baby. What defines bottom-up attention is that it is something we can't avoid noticing.

Top-down attention, on the other hand, occurs only when we prompt ourselves to look for something. For example, an instructional coach gathering data on the different questions a teacher asks might miss some questions if something distracting happens in class. With top-down attention, we must be intentional to notice what we notice. If we don't tell ourselves to see whatever we are looking for, we miss it.

In our lives at work and home, negative experiences often catch our bottom-up attention. One research volunteer discovered this when she practiced being a witness to the good. "We tend to look for more negative than positive," she wrote. To authentically share positive information, she said, "requires thought and intentional action." To truly be witnesses to the good, we need to teach ourselves to see all that is going well and not just the aberrations; in other words, we need to use top-down attention.

Direct, Specific, Nonattributive Comments. Harvard researchers Robert Kegan and Lisa Lahey (2001) offer a second suggestion on how to share positive information, which they refer to as "a language of ongoing regard." A "language of ongoing regard" has specific characteristics. Kegan and Lahey stress that authentic appreciative or admiring feedback needs to be (a) direct, (b) specific, and (c) nonattributive. Most people recognize the importance of direct, specific feedback. Direct comments are spoken to a person in the first person, not about a person, in the third person. Thus, it is preferable to tell someone directly, "I appreciate your help," rather than saying publicly, "I appreciate Jean's help."

Specific comments clearly explain the details of what we are praising, rather than offering general statements. One participant focused on this skill, and recorded many specific comments on her reflection form, such as, "I notice he is responding more positively to you during special time," and "Jackson was a lot less frustrated after you helped him with his laptop."

The importance of making nonattributive comments may be less obvious. Kegan and Lahey in *How the Way We Talk Can Change the Way We Work: Seven Languages for Transformation* (2001) explain that our positive comments about others are more effective when we describe our experience of others rather than the attributes of others. For example, it is less effective to say to someone, "You're a kind teacher" (describing an attribute that we judge them to have) than it is to say, "Three students have told me that they can tell you really care about them." Kegan and Lahey explain why nonattributive feedback is more effective:

> It may seem odd to you that we're urging you not to make statements of this sort: "Carlos, I just want you to know how much I appreciate how generous you are" (or: "what a good sense of humor you have" or "that you always know the right thing to say"), or "Alice, you are so patient" (or, "so prompt," "so never-say-die," "always there when you are needed,"), and so on . . . These seem like such nice things to say to someone . . . The problem we see is this: the person, inevitably and quite properly, relates what you say to how she knows herself to be. You can tell Carlos he is generous, but he knows how generous he actually is. You can tell Alice she is very patient, but she knows her side of how patient she is being with you. (p. 99)

Learning how to give direct, specific, nonattributive feedback is a skill that every person should develop, and one that can be practiced and developed daily until it becomes a habit of thought. We can practice developing this "language of ongoing regard" at the workplace, but we can also practice it with our children, parents, spouse, or other people in their lives. There is great benefit in practicing such feedback until it becomes a habitual way of communicating. Indeed, it seems strange that we often feel uncomfortable telling people directly and specifically why we appreciate them. Perhaps we're afraid our comments will seem to be insincere or self-serving flattery. Nothing could be further from the truth. As Kegan and Lahey (2001) state, "Ongoing regard is not about praising, stroking, or positively defining a person to herself or to others. We say again: it is about enhancing the quality of a precious kind of information. It is about informing the person about *our* experience of him or her" (p. 101).

Growth and Fixed Mindset. Carol Dweck's research on praise, which she summarizes in her frequently cited book *Mindset: The New Psychology of Success* (2006), further enriches our understanding of how to be a witness to the good. In an interview published on www.highlightspar ents.com, she summarized her findings:

> Parents must stop praising their children's intelligence. My research has shown that, far from boosting children's self-esteem, it makes them more fragile and can undermine their motivation and learning. Praising children's intelligence puts them in a fixed mindset, makes them afraid of making mistakes, and makes them lose their confidence when something is hard for them. Instead, parents should praise the process—their children's effort, strategy, perseverance, or improvement. Then the children will be willing to take on challenges and will know how to stick with things—even the hard ones.

To be a witness to the good, then, sounds like a fairly complex task. Our "language of ongoing regard" must be authentic, direct, specific, and nonattributive, and focus on effort rather than intelligence. This does not mean that we should worry about the nuances of every comment we make before we say anything. What matters is this. First, we must communicate to others that we see the good they are doing. Our comments must be real, for otherwise they may backfire. But if we criticize others more than we encourage them, job one is to turn that around. Second, after we have developed the habit of noticing and communicating what we see going well, we can work at refining our language—striving to focus on effort, rather than fixed traits, and using specific, direct, nonattributive comments.

There is an interesting video on YouTube. In the video, a mother encourages her blind son to step off a curb for the first time. If you read a transcript of her comments, you'd say her praise was very poorly crafted. She says such general comments as, "You can do it" and "Good job." But when you watch the video, you see that her words tell her son something important. Her message is that she is there with her son, he shouldn't be afraid, she loves him, believes in him, and is proud of him. The video shows that the message is more important than how we say it. We shouldn't wait until we have the perfect words when have something important to say.

GETTING BETTER AT BEING A WITNESS TO THE GOOD

To improve at being a witness to the good, we simply need to try to improve the quality of our comments, and then monitor whether or not the way we share information changes the way people respond to our comments. The most important thing is to be intentional about positive comments, and three forms are included at the end of this chapter to help you do that.

The *Looking Back: Being a Witness to the Good* form can be used to review conversations we've recorded so we can assess how effectively we shared positive information and to identify how we can improve as we strive to be a witness to the good.

The *Looking At: Being a Witness to the Good* form can be used to clarify in your own mind what it looks like to be a witness to the good.

The *Looking Ahead: Being a Witness to the Good* form can be used to think through the positive comments we wish to

Sometimes I focus on the negative, but this process has taught me how to find the good in every situation. There really is more good than bad in most of our everyday encounters.

—**Lisa Sligh,**
Educational Consultant,
Baltimore,
Maryland

share, in particular to plan how to provide direct, specific, nonattributive, positive feedback.

TO SUM UP

John Gottman and Joan DeClaire (2001) and their research colleagues have spent decades monitoring the way people react, and they have found that the most important variable in relationships is emotional connection. Their research has identified some critical variables that stand at the heart of emotional connection. If we learn about those variables, and adapt our behavior, we can build more emotional connection into our lives. The variables they identify are the following:

- **A Bid:** Can be a question, a gesture, a look, a touch—any single expression that says, "I want to be connected to you." (p. 4)
- **Turning Toward:** Means to react in positive ways to another's bids for emotional connection. (p. 16)
- **Turning Away:** This pattern of relating generally involves ignoring another's bid or acting preoccupied. (p. 17)
- **Turning Against:** People who turn against one another's bids for connection might be described as belligerent or argumentative. For example, if a man fantasized about owning a passing sports car, his friend might reply, "On your salary? Dream on!" (p. 17)

One important and powerful way in which we connect with other people is by sharing positive information. However, frequently we do not share positive information as effectively as we could.

One reason we struggle to share positive information effectively is that our normal ways of perceiving make it difficult for us to see what is going well. Winifred Gallagher (2009) identifies two different types of attention:

- Bottom-up attention is the attention we use when we see something we can't help noticing.
- Top-down attention is the attention we use when we have to prompt ourselves to look for something.

Being a witness to the good requires top-down attention.

Kegan and Lahey have identified three characteristics that are required for effectively sharing positive information. A "language of ongoing regard" shared effectively is

- Direct
- Specific
- Nonattributive

GOING DEEPER

John Gottman's books about relationships are all worth reading. I first encountered his ideas by reading *The Relationship Cure: A Five Step Guide to Strengthening Your Marriage, Family, and Friendships* (2001), which he coauthored with Joan DeClaire. This book provides a broad overview of Gottman's findings and how they relate to all relationships.

Gottman's two books on marriage, *The Seven Principles for Making Marriage Work: A Practical Guide From the Country's Foremost Relationship Expert* (1999) with Nan Silver and *10 Lessons to Transform Your Marriage* (2006) with Julie Schwartz, provide valuable strategies couples can use to build a marriage that thrives. My wife Jenny and I also attended the marriage workshop offered by John and Julie Gottman, and we highly recommend the experience for couples who are interested in strengthening their marriage.

Paul Ekman's work on facial expressions, especially as they are described in *Emotions Revealed, Second Edition: Recognizing Faces and Feelings to Improve Communication and Emotional Life* (2007), is a fascinating look at what Ekman sees as the universal language of facial expressions. Ekman's book helps us better understand how micro expressions, facial expressions that last less than a second, can convey an enormous amount of information.

Winifred Gallagher's book *Rapt: Attention and the Focused Life* (2009) is a very interesting and helpful description of how our attention works in ways that we do not realize. An intentional life is an aware life, and Gallagher's book helps us better understand how we see the world.

Edward Hallowell's *Shine: Using Brain Science to Get the Best From Your People* (2011) offers a compelling argument for each of us to try and connect with others.

Kegan and Lahey's *How the Way We Talk Can Change the Way We Work: Seven Languages for Transformation* (2001) taught me more about sharing positive information than any book I've read, and what they say about that topic is only a small part of their very useful and interesting book.

LOOKING BACK:

Making Emotional Connections

Record yourself in a conversation. This could be personal or professional. Point the camera toward your conversation partner, as long as he or she agrees. After, watch the video carefully to see whether you or your partner (a) made bids, (b) turned toward, (c) turned away, or (d) turned against. Pay particular attention to nonverbal communication.

When did you see your partner make a bid, turn toward, away from, or against one of your bids?

....

....

....

....

When did you miss opportunities to makes bids to your partner or turn toward your partner's bids?

....

....

....

....

When did you see yourself or your partner turn away from or against a bid?

....

....

....

....

....

LOOKING AT:

Making Emotional Connections

(1 of 2)

///

PEOPLE WATCHING

Take 30 minutes to watch people around you and observe how they
(a) make bids, (b) turn toward, (c) turn away, or (d) turn against. Pay
particular attention to nonverbal communication.

What examples of bids did you see?

....
....

How did you see people turn toward bids?

....
....

What did they do that opened up or closed down the conversation?

....
....

How did you see people turn away from bids?

....
....

How did you see people turn against bids?

....
....

LOOKING AT:

Making Emotional Connections

(2 of 2)

EMOTIONAL BIDS

Use this form to record the emotional bids you make each day. Use it whenever you want to remind yourself to make more bids. You only need include a few words to record the bid, such as, "offered to get coffee for Alex." The purpose of the form is to prompt you to make numerous bids for emotional connection. Don't spend more than a few seconds noting each bid. You may want to carry this form with you and just write down what occurs.

DATE	BID

LOOKING AHEAD:

Making Emotional Connections

Identify someone you think you especially need to connect with more effectively.

What can you do to make more bids?

What can you do to turn toward more effectively?

What can you do to be more mindful of people's need to connect?

What else can you do to build an emotional connection with your partner?

LOOKING BACK:

Being a Witness to the Good

Record yourself in a conversation during which you share positive information. This could be a personal or professional conversation. After, watch the video to analyze how effectively you were a witness to the good.

Note the praise you gave your partner below, and identify the attributes of your praise:

COMMENTS	ATTRIBUTIVE	NONATTRIBUTIVE	SPECIFIC	DIRECT	INDIRECT
	○	○	○	○	○
	○	○	○	○	○
	○	○	○	○	○
	○	○	○	○	○
	○	○	○	○	○
	○	○	○	○	○
	○	○	○	○	○
	○	○	○	○	○
	○	○	○	○	○
	○	○	○	○	○
	○	○	○	○	○

What should you do differently (if anything) to share positive information more effectively in the future?

LOOKING AT:

Being a Witness to the Good

Describe a time when someone shared some positive feedback with you that really had a positive impact on you.

....

....

....

....

....

What was it about that feedback that made it so effective?

....

....

....

....

....

What can you learn from that experience about how you can be a witness to the good?

....

....

....

....

....

LOOKING AHEAD:

Being a Witness to the Good

Use this form to prepare yourself for a conversation you are soon to have where you intend to be a witness to the good.

What general praise would you give to your partner?

_____

_____

_____

_____

What evidence supports your positive observation?

_____

_____

_____

_____

What can you do to make it more specific?

_____

_____

_____

_____

Finding Common Ground

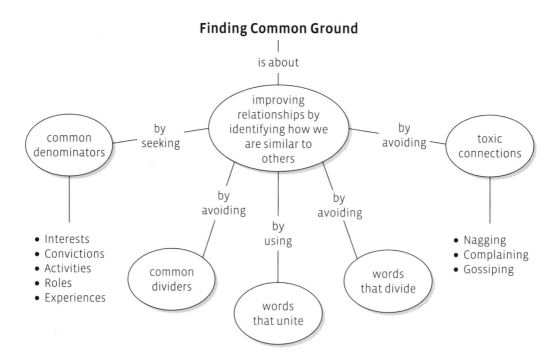

is about

improving relationships by identifying how we are similar to others

by seeking — common denominators
- Interests
- Convictions
- Activities
- Roles
- Experiences

by avoiding — common dividers

by using — words that unite

by avoiding — words that divide

by avoiding — toxic connections
- Nagging
- Complaining
- Gossiping

FINDING COMMON GROUND

I note the obvious differences between each sort and type, but we are more alike, my friends, than we are unalike.

—From "Human Family,"
by Maya Angelou (1991)

We all want to be heard, understood, respected, and shown compassion. Very few people are really out to destroy others. They are out there, but they are acting that way because they feel threatened. It is hard to feel threatened when you feel similar to another person or when you recognize you may belong in some way to the same way of thinking, feeling, or doing.

—Jennifer Stadum,
Indian Education for All Specialist,
State of Montana Office of Public Interest,
Bozeman, Montana

For much of the last decade, my son Geoff and his wife Jenny have lived in the Mufindi Highlands of Tanzania, where they lead a charity dedicated to improving the lives of children who live in extreme poverty and who, in most cases, have lost their parents to HIV. Geoff's organization makes a huge difference, and I have seen first-hand that they truly save lives almost every week.[1]

---

[1]You can learn more about the work Geoff and Jenny do in Tanzania by visiting www.mufindiorphans.org.

Geoff has a gift for learning languages, and as soon as he moved to Tanzania, he started to learn the local ways of communicating. First, he mastered Kiswahili, and then Kihehe, the tribal language spoken in the Mufindi region where he lived. "My goal," Geoff told me, "is to be able to say at least a few words in every tribal language in Tanzania."

The Mufindi Highlands of Tanzania are a long way from Lawrence, Kansas, but I have been able to visit Geoff and Jenny and their family a few times. The drive to Mufindi from the main airport in Dar Es Saalam is a 14-hour marathon. On one occasion when Geoff was driving me back to the airport, a white-uniformed police officer flagged Geoff down as Geoff drove us through a village.

The officer walked up to Geoff's window, and, without even saying hello, barked at Geoff: "I'm going to fine you 400,000 shillings (at that time about $150.00) for driving 70 kilometers per hour in 50 kilometer zone."

Geoff explained quickly that he didn't realize the speed limit had changed. The officer barked back, "You didn't see the sign? I'm going to fine you another 400,000 shillings for not watching for the sign." At this point, Geoff was very worried about all the money he might have to pay since he was living on a volunteer's budget, and I was very worried about all the movies I'd seen about prisons in the developing world.

Geoff got out of the truck at that point, and he and the officer began to talk. I watched as the officer's facial expression and posture changed. The officer relaxed and smiled, then he and Geoff laughed together, and I knew things would be okay. Geoff soon got back in his truck and we were back on the road.

As we took off, Geoff told me what had happened. When Geoff shook hands with the officer, he asked him where he was from. When the officer told Geoff he was from Sumbawanga, Geoff spoke to him in his tribal language, Kifipa. Startled to hear his own language instead of English, the officer smiled and told Geoff, "No white man has ever spoken to me in my language before." The officer let Geoff off with a warning, and even gave Geoff his cell phone number in case Geoff might need help in the future. A few months later, Geoff's wife had her computer stolen in a local coffee shop, and Geoff called the officer for help. The officer quickly located Jenny's computer and she had it back that day—all because Geoff found common ground with the officer.

Finding common ground is an important habit to adopt so that we can have better conversations. When we find common ground, we move beyond our differences, and we communicate that we truly see someone else. In this way, finding common ground is a way to show respect. One volunteer in our study described how finding common ground was profoundly changing how she related to the people in her school.

> I am connecting with teachers on such a deeper level. I remember someone saying to me, "I want to see God on everyone's face." I am now having that experience. It is connecting me to teachers at such a deeper level. I know this for sure: I am going to explore this more. Since we are connecting and we are exploring practices to move students and teachers forward, the teachers and I have become inspired. Our inspiration motivates us to want to do the good work.

Finding common ground, as one volunteer wrote, "gets the other person more engaged in the conversation." And as another volunteer wrote, "finding common ground is immensely important if meaningful, productive conversations are to occur." Indeed, to seek what we share in common with another person, as a point of departure for conversation, is a radical act in today's polarized world. Day after day, we see people do exactly the opposite; rather than finding common ground, people highlight and obsess over their obvious differences.

Today, the United States seems to be polarized by discussions around moral, religious, and especially political issues. Topics like gun control, health care, the president's foreign policy, gay marriage, and abortion can trigger incredibly hostile conversations. And our media seems to fan the fire. On the news programs we watch, the comments that get played are not the quiet moments of respect and agreement, but the loud statements of almost childish hostility. The more outlandish and insensitive the comment, it seems, the more likely it will show up on our Facebook page.

I have found that common ground *always* exists somewhere. Sometimes it is hard to find, but when it is, that is because of my focus. I have also seen, especially with people that I have a more strained relationship with, that finding common ground helps to tear down walls, and helps to build relationships. The roadblocks are self-imposed. When I don't focus on finding common ground, it doesn't happen. When I forget about it, the conversation suffers, but when I really try to find it, I always can.

—Research volunteer

In *Healing the Heart of Democracy: The Courage to Create a Politics Worthy of the Human Spirit* (2001), Parker Palmer describes how our time is dominated by what he calls "the politics of rage." Palmer reports on a study by David Gal and David Rucker that found that when people are "shown solid evidence contradicting their most fundamental beliefs," they often become "more forceful in advocating those beliefs" (p. 16). All around us we see our leaders attack each other, while television programs further heighten the anger in the rhetoric simply to get more viewers to watch their programs. All the more reason, I contend then, for us to stand against the politics of rage by striving to find common ground with others, especially those who see the world differently than we do.

The Psychology of Separateness: Why It Is So Hard to See Similarities

One reason we need to strive to find common ground—and why we struggle to do so—is that other people simply do not understand the very clear and simple things we say. One of the major barriers to finding common ground, and communication in general, is the perceptual errors (including our own) people make that stand in the way of clear communication.

People are meaning-making beings, and when they see something about another person that they do not understand, they often find ways to explain away their confusion. Meaning, in other words, exists in the minds of our conversation partners as much as it resides in our brains, and unfortunately, the meaning others make about what we communicate can be wrong. Psychologists have identified many perceptual errors that can lead us to unknowingly misunderstand what we see and experience. A few perceptual errors that most inhibit finding common ground are described below.

CONFIRMATION BIAS

One reason people may not see what they hold in common with others is confirmation bias. In *Decisive: How to Make Better Choices in Life and Work,* Chip and Dan Heath

(2013) describe confirmation bias as our natural tendency to seek data that support our assumptions:

> Our normal habit in life is to develop a quick belief about a situation and then seek out information that bolsters our belief . . . Researchers have found this result again and again. When people have the opportunity to collect information from the world, they are more likely to select information that supports their preexisting attitudes, beliefs, and actions. (p. 11)

The tendency to seek out support for our own beliefs is a major reason people do not see what they hold in common with others. For example, a person with either a conservative or progressive political perspective might have a negative opinion of those who hold an opposite political opinion, and then see every action those other persons do through the political lens. The result is that even when colleagues could find common ground, they fail to see it since they are so focused on their differences. As one research volunteer wrote on her reflection sheet, "It's a lot easier to find common ground with people who say what you want to hear."

HABITUATION

A second reason many people misread others stems from a phenomenon psychologists refer to as habituation— the fact that we lose our sensitivity to just about anything we experience repeatedly. Through habituation, we can become desensitized to any experience, pleasant or unpleasant, beautiful or ugly. This means that what at one time would have been impossible not to see can eventually become practically invisible.

The impact of habituation is that over time we can lose sight of all that we share with others. Many of the volunteers in our study talked about, as one person wrote on her reflection form, "that we are all here for the same reason: to help students and support their learning." Over time, though, because of habituation, we can forget about all we hold in common and let our few differences keep us from moving forward in meaningful ways.

PRIMACY EFFECT

Primacy effect occurs when our first experiences with someone bias us in favor of a particular impression of that person. For example, when I had my first game on a co-ed softball team, I hit a long homerun during my first at bat. That day I was pegged as the cleanup hitter, even though ground balls to the shortstop were more my typical style. It took about a month, and far too many double plays, before my teammates realized that homeruns would come few and far between when I was at bat.

The primacy effect can significantly interfere with other people's abilities to read us. As Heidi Grant Halvorson has written in *No One Understands You and What to Do About It* (2015), "The primacy effect is almost entirely responsible for the fact that sometimes, we can do no wrong in someone else's eyes, while at other times, we seem to be screwed no matter what we do" (p. 25).

STEREOTYPES

Stereotypes are a particularly tricky form of perceptual error. Grant Halvorson, again, writes that

> Stereotypes are the beliefs we have about categories of people, and we categorize people in lots of ways: by gender, race, sexual orientation, ethnicity, profession, and socioeconomic class. Some of the beliefs associated with these categories are positive, such as *Asians are good at math* or *firefighters are brave*. Others are decidedly less so (e.g., *redheads are hot-tempered; women are weak; poor people are lazy*). (p. 29; italics in original)

Stereotypes are attractive because they reduce cognitive load, which is the amount of brainpower we need to use to do something. As a t-shirt I saw in an airport stated, "Stereotypes are a real time saver." The problem, of course, is that stereotypes can lead to racist, homophobic, sexist, or other dehumanizing beliefs that lead us to see others as being part of a group and blind us to each individual's characteristics.

Stereotypes also interfere with finding common ground. When we see another person as a stereotype, we do not see them for who they really are, and that makes it very difficult for us to see what we share. If I don't really know you, how can I know what we have in common? When we truly seek out what we hold in common, we can shatter stereotypes and come to see that the person we had dismissed as a type is actually an awful lot like us. As Parker Palmer writes in *Healing the Heart of Democracy* (2011), "The more you know about another person's story, the less possible it is to see that person as your enemy" (p. 5).

There are dozens of other perceptual errors that have been identified by psychologists, including the "halo effect," our tendency to be biased by our perception of people having one attribute (e.g., good-looking people are smart); the "worse than average effect," the tendency to think we are worse than others at tasks (despite the fact that there is no evidence to support that view); and even the "IKEA effect," the tendency to overvalue the worth of furniture we have put together ourselves. What perceptual errors show is that when people read what we say and do, they will make their own meaning out of what they don't understand about us, and often they will get us wrong. For that reason, to ensure that people do understand us, and to break through invisible barriers between us and others, we need to find common ground.

> I recognize that, although our personalities, our viewpoints, and our motives may differ vastly, we can connect with one another. Fundamentally, we all need to protect our spirit and feel that we have those two keystones to good relationships, choice and voice. If no other common ground exists, *those needs* are primordial in the human race. And, now that I really think about it, if only we could meet and honor those ancient and abiding needs in each other, *that* might be the only common ground we truly need to establish.
>
> **—Carol Walker,**
> Instructional Coach,
> Green River,
> Wyoming

Strategies for Finding Common Ground

Volunteers in our study who experimented with finding common ground saw the importance of implementing the habit in all kinds of situations. For some, finding common ground was an important way to build connections with other educators in schools. Volunteers wrote about finding common ground around "learning new curriculum and synthesizing old and new approaches," "struggles with students, especially behavior," and, as Carolyn Matteson wrote on her reflection form, "the deep desire everyone feels to do the best they can for and with students." Matteson added, "the motive to serve students provided the common denominator I needed to get me to listen to others' points of view when we talked about a topic that I have strong feelings about."

I believe that I need to cultivate patience in conversations. I seem to have become a more results-oriented person as I've grown older, and in my determination to eliminate barriers to our work (basically by being a heat-seeking missile), I wonder if I may be cutting myself off from understanding my colleagues as well as they deserve. There is such a strong drive within me, and maybe in many people, to be competitive and to achieve results. I do want results, but I wonder if I am allowing others to feel honored and happy.

—**Carol Walker,**
Instructional Coach,
Green River,
Wyoming

For many, the common bonds they found with others related to experiences they had outside school. When Sherry Eichinger discovered she shared interests in running and cooking with a fellow teacher, it made it easier for them to talk. Others found common ground in talking about their past work experiences (both had worked in urban settings), pregnancy, shopping, shoes, marriage, and even cheddar popcorn. Common ground provided an opening for many different types of conversations. As one volunteer wrote, "My grandmother taught me that we all laugh, cry, and love in the same way. Her wise words have served me well as I have tried to find common ground."

What was most striking about the many notes people wrote about their experiments with common ground was that they found the habit to be absolutely vital for some of their most important conversations. People wrote about finding common ground when talking with their 87-year-old father about moving into a retirement home, trying to convince a teacher not to quit the profession, talking with a friend about the death of one of her parents, and talking with a 21-year-old son about why life is truly worth living. Common ground made many important conversations possible.

Finding common ground is essential because, as one volunteer wrote, "there has to be common ground for a relationship to exist." Fortunately, there are simple strategies you can employ, and that were tested by many people in our study, to find common ground. Those strategies are (a) commit to finding common ground; (b) seek common denominators, avoid common dividers; (c) use words that unite, avoid words that divide; and (d) avoid toxic connections.

COMMIT TO FINDING COMMON GROUND

The first step in finding common ground is simply to commit to do it. The core belief in this strategy is that, as Maya Angelou wrote in her poem "Human Family," "we are more alike than we are unalike." Therefore, in every interaction, we should attempt to find common ground, especially with those who are or appear to be different from us. The creators of the Milestone Project, an organization dedicated to visually showing how much we each have in common with the rest of humanity, have developed a pledge that both children and adults can embrace. The pledge puts in words what a commitment to finding common ground might look like.

Many of the volunteers in our study reported that the simple act of planning to find common ground significantly increased the likelihood that it would happen. As Marilyn Allen wrote, "It seems to me that whenever a person plans to find common ground at the outset, they will almost certainly be more successful at doing these things. By setting an intention, by identifying these goals prior to a conversation, it is like a guarantee that you will be more successful in achieving these outcomes."

SEEK COMMON DENOMINATORS

Another way to find common ground is to consciously look for similarities we share with our conversation partners. I have organized those possible similarities around the acronym I-CARE (Interests, Convictions, Activities, Roles, and Experiences) so that it will be easy to remember during conversations when you wish to find common ground. Seeking out I-CARE commonalities can be a point of departure for many conversations. One volunteer wrote, "I've developed a curiosity about finding common ground that I didn't have before. I like the challenge of finding common ground when I first meet someone—it's kind of a thrill for me when I recognize common ground for the first time."

Interests. Many participants wrote about finding common interests that they shared with others. For some, shared interests had to do with their work as educators. Janette Cochran wrote about talking with another teacher who shared her love for *The Frame Routine* developed by Ed Ellis. Others talked about their common goal of providing support for parents, or teachers, or students. For many in our study, the common ground was found outside school. Jenni Donohoo wrote about finding common ground when talking about husbands and shopping. Sidra Scharff talked about finding common ground when talking about music with a student. Other common interests might be passions such as particular books, food, local restaurants, or sports teams.

The Milestone Pledge

1. I pledge to notice the way people are like me before I notice the ways they are different.

2. I pledge to say only kind things to others and to stop myself before I say mean things.

3. I pledge to use respectful words to work out my problems with other people.

4. I pledge to encourage my friends to do these things too because...I know that if everyone does these four things, we will put an end to intolerance and hatred all over the world. (Steckel & Steckel, 2010)

Convictions. The most common conviction people shared was a commitment to students. When Jenny Gunja started to look for common ground, she found common beliefs about "politics and government, cultural heritage, dancing, movies, immigration reform, family, teaching urban youth, coaching, professional development, and budget cuts." Chris Slocum wrote about her team's common commitment to quality professional work. "We don't take this lightly. We want to do a professional job and provide powerful and easy-to-implement strategies for our teachers. We share many of the same values—saving teachers time, helping deliver useful information to teachers, improving teacher instruction to benefit students, and so forth." Other convictions or beliefs that surfaced were related to religion, ideas, and general principles of living.

Activities. Many participants in our study found common ground around activities that they enjoyed. For many, those activities were a big part of their daily routine. This was especially true for those who shared their passion for fitness, running, or a healthy lifestyle. Others wrote about finding a shared love for cooking, or baking, or even watching particular televisions shows. Some of the other activities that people found they had in common were singing, writing, or leading groups (such as youth groups) in their communities and places of worship.

Roles. Greg Netzger and his wife are both school principals, and because they share common jobs, Greg says they "almost always have something to talk about." Such was the case for many volunteers in our project. When they discovered they shared a role with someone else, they had many points of departure for conversation. Teachers, adjunct professors, specialists, and coaches shared with each other the rewards, challenges, and even the loneliness of their roles. Others talked about their roles outside schools, including such roles as parent, daughter or son, committee member, scout leader, or choir leader. When people found they shared a role with someone else, they often found they suddenly had an awful lot to talk about.

Experiences. Sometimes, a shared experience can be a powerful link between people. Volunteers in our study wrote about the connections that developed when they realized they had traveled to the same places (London and Paris at the top of the list). Others talked about working for the same principals or in the same schools, or jobs they've had—including selling ice cream in the 1980s. Other experiences people shared included people they have known, universities they have attended, or experiences related to being a husband or wife, or simply living day-to-day, like going to the beach. Shared experiences included everything from trips to Broadway to traveling around the country to watching the Grateful Dead.

AVOID COMMON DIVIDERS

When we find something we share with another person, it can be the steppingstone to establishing an authentic connection or relationship. However, if we call attention to a major difference between us and our conversation partners, it can build a stone wall between us.

Interestingly, all of the potential common denominators listed above (interests, convictions, activities, roles, experiences) can also be dividers. An obvious example of this is political beliefs. If you and I have the same political bumper sticker on our car, we can probably find a common bond in our shared political views. But if we have different bumper stickers supporting different parties, we may have a little difficulty relating when that difference surfaces. In situations where we have obvious differences, we need to be especially intentional about seeking common ground.

Even trivial issues, like which college basketball team we cheer for, can become dividers. I have had people come to my presentations and say that their spouse told them not to come because I worked at the University of Kansas, a rival to their spouse's basketball team. The challenge is to seek what we have in common first, before we address our differences—not to be upset by our different teams, but to be united in our appreciation of the sport itself.

Common dividers, when they become personal, can deeply separate people, even those who love each other. One of the volunteers in our study described how politics had divided her and her mother. "I told my mother, 'I don't like talking about this with you. I don't like talking to

The Milestones Project is an organization that is dedicated to visually showing how much we each have in common with the rest of humanity. Founded by photographers Richard and Michele Steckel (2010), the project assembles photographs of children from around the world to show, as they say, "a world where what divides us is healed and what unites us is loved by seeing how we are all the same." Their photographs can be found at www .milestonesproject .com.

people who have different views than me. I can't believe you support that law. It's racist. It encourages prejudice—there is no other way to look at it. I don't want to come to your house for breakfast if there is going to be tension. I just don't understand you.'"

Like this volunteer in our study, many of us don't like "talking to people who have different views." But this is the real challenge we face. To overcome the polarization and divisiveness that is at epidemic levels in some locations, we need to start by finding what we hold in common. As Parker Palmer has written, the challenge we face—to see what we hold in common with others with whom we differ—is the same challenge Abraham Lincoln described in his first inaugural speech on March 4, 1861:

> We are not enemies, but friends. We must not be enemies. Though passion may have strained it must not break our bonds of affection. The mystic chords of memory, stretching from every battle field and patriot grave to every living heart and hearthstone all over this broad land, will yet swell the chorus of the Union, when again touch, as surely they will be, by the better angels of our nature. (as cited in Palmer, 2011, p. 27)

USE WORDS THAT UNITE; AVOID WORDS THAT DIVIDE

Words have the power to bring people together or push them apart. To find common ground, we should use words that unite and avoid words that divide. The most fundamental word choice is to say *we* instead of *I*, *yes* instead of *no*, and *and* instead of *but*.

Volunteers in our global study of communication kept track of the words they used when they acted to find common ground. Generally, their choice of words can be organized into single words or phrases. The words that people recorded communicated unity and demonstrated that people shared the experiences of their conversation partners. Thus, people wrote that they used the words *me too, yes exactly, I understand, wow,* and *us.* One person wrote that she was careful to replace the word *help* with *collaborate.* Many of the words communicated hope, including *love, God, family, team, together,* and *thank you.*

Participants in our project also shared phrases they said built common ground. The phrases validated others and communicated unity. Some examples include "That's what we do," "Have you experienced ___?," "We could ___," "What do you think about ___?," "I'm here for you," "So do I," and "You have every reason to expect that." One person wrote that she felt a common bond with a teacher she was coaching when the teacher said, "You make me a better person."

Using words that unite is important, but a second part of this strategy is avoiding words that carry negative emotional implications. For example, words like *careless*, *dishonest*, *lazy*, and *unprofessional* can be very divisive when directed at others—even when they are used indirectly. To say to someone, "It would be dishonest to say that," is not much different from telling someone, "You're lying." We must avoid such language and continually look for language that unifies.

> A useful online resource is "Forty Inviting Comments" and "Forty Disinviting Comments" identified by William Watson Purkey and John M. Novak (n.d.) at their website *Forty Successes:* http://www.mysdcc.sdccd.edu/Staff/Instructor_Development/Content/HTML/Forty_Successes.htm.

AVOID TOXIC CONNECTIONS

For most of us, the connection that comes from finding common ground generates very positive emotions. We like it, and we feel good when we connect with others. We need to be careful, however, not to assume that all connections are good connections. Some kinds of connection can be counterproductive and even toxic. As one volunteer in the study wrote, "I've experienced lots of good things, but also some disturbing ones. Most disturbing was how easy it was to unite around negative things." Simply put, there are two kinds of common ground—one is healthy; the other is not.

Unhealthy or toxic connection involves any kind of common ground that diminishes others. This type of talk is not good for the community or workplace, is demeaning to others, and diminishes our own sense of self. Perhaps even worse, toxic comments spread like an unhealthy virus. Kegan and Lahey, in their book *How the Way We Talk Can Change the Way We Work* (2001), describe the unhealthy impact that can come from toxic connections.

> The language of complaining, wishing, and hoping is a highly frequented conversational form, but it . . . [does not foster] . . . personal learning and

reflective leadership . . . [and] complaining grows on its own—and it grows everywhere just like a weed. (p. 20)

The quick hit of pleasure that comes from criticizing a boss or gossiping about a peer usually carries its own punishment. When we engage in toxic connection, we are at least partially aware that we are being duplicitous, that who we are with one person is not who we are with others. When people realize their lack of authenticity, that they are not treating others the way they would like to be treated, it can significantly lower their self-esteem. As Parker Palmer (2011) has written, "There are times when the heart, like the canary in a coal mine, breathes in the world's toxicity and begins to die" (p. 3).

Toxic connections should be avoided, and Chapter 8 describes strategies we can use to redirect toxic conversations. But positive connections can move us much closer to better conversations. Finding Common Ground is a habit to build unity with others by seeing positive ways in which we are alike. It is an attempt to connect with others, especially others who, on the surface, seem a lot different from us.

Finding common ground holds great promise for strengthening relationships, but it will not work if it is done in an insincere way. To find common ground is to see others clearly, and then to share how we are similar. Finding common ground is not a cheap trick to build connection, but rather a way to respect and validate those with whom we interact—especially those who hold views that are different than our own.

Finally, "finding" common ground is not the same as "telling" others we share the same goals, or objectives. When we are finding common ground, we never begin a sentence with "I know we can all agree . . . ," which is a rhetorical way of saying, "Let's do it my way." Finding common ground is about what we hold in common, but it is also a mutual exploration, a mutual discovery. We do it together, not to each other, and that is part of the reason finding common ground can have such a positive impact on relationships. By finding common ground, we open authentic doors to communication, connection, and meaningful relationship; we seek out what William Orville Douglas calls "the common ground binding all mankind together."

The videos created by the filmmakers at Playing for Change powerfully illustrate the idea that we hold much in common with everyone else in the world. The artists at Playing for Change create short movies by filming people all over the world playing the same songs, and then they edit the recordings to create the impression that everyone is playing the song together at the same time. You can view the videos at www .playingforchange .com.

Getting Better at Finding Common Ground

Often, the first thing we need to do if we want to find common ground is to recognize and abandon any existing judgments about others that might interfere with our ability to find common ground. Something as simple as another person's allegiance to a sports team that is a rival to our team can get in the way of seeing how much we are similar to others.

Once we have done our best to clear our heads of judgments, our task is simply to try the habit and see what happens. To help with this, I have created the acronym I-CARE. Of course, acronyms can be annoying. They can be too cute and simplistic and they can dumb down ideas so much that they lose their power. In this case, though, the purpose of the acronym is to provide a simple memory hook so that at the start of any conversation, we can have in mind many different ways we can seek out common ground. If it seems silly to call up the acronym in your mind as you meet people and talk, then don't do it, but many people have found the acronym to be a valuable point of departure for conversations.

To develop the habit of finding common ground, I suggest you memorize the acronym and then try it with as many people as you can. Try it with coworkers, students, family members, cab drivers, hair stylists or barbers, or pretty much anyone you meet. I suggest you especially try it with people with whom you feel you have little in common.

When you try to find common ground, pay attention to what happens during the conversation. Are you able to find common ground? If so, do you feel more positive about your conversation partner? Does anything make it difficult for you to find common ground? Does anything make it easier to find common ground?

To help you find common ground, as with all of the other habits, I have created reflection forms you can use to help you make these ideas become habits.

Use the *Looking Back: Finding Common Ground* form to reflect on a conversation after it is over. In the best situations, you might review an audio or video conversation that

---

Strategies for Finding Common Ground

1. Commit to finding common ground.

2. Find common denominators, avoid common dividers.

3. Use words that unite; avoid words that divide.

4. Avoid toxic connections.

had some other purpose (for example, a coaching conversation), and then consider how effectively you implemented the habit. In most cases, you will need to use this form even when there is no recording of the conversation, just to consider what worked and what still needs to improve as you try to find common ground.

Use the *Looking At: Finding Common Ground (1 of 2)* form to keep track of the interactions you had where you attempted to find common ground. Note the interaction, what you did, and the outcome. The purpose of the form is to help you be more aware of what happens when you attempt to find common ground.

Use the *Looking At: Finding Common Ground (2 of 2)* form to experiment with the I-CARE model for finding common ground. This form might be used by members of a team who are learning the Better Conversations Beliefs and Habits or by two people who are learning together.

Use the *Looking Ahead: Finding Common Ground* form to plan how you will find common ground with someone during an upcoming conversation. This form might be especially useful when you are planning an important meeting, or when you are first attempting to use this habit.

TO SUM UP

Finding Common Ground is a powerful communication habit we can use to improve our relationships and communicate more effectively. It is also a noble act that makes the world a better place.

We can employ four simple strategies to help us find common ground.

- Seek common denominators and avoid common dividers. We can do this by remembering the I-CARE acronym—Interests, Convictions, Activities, Roles, Experiences.
- Avoid common dividers, which is to say keep the I-CARE acronym in mind to avoid topics that might put a barrier between us and others. Once common ground has been found, it will be much easier to discuss where we disagree.

- Use words that unite and avoid words that divide by monitoring what you say to ensure that your words don't become a barrier to understanding.
- Avoid toxic connections such as nagging, complaining, gossiping, and so forth. Conversations that diminish others are never healthy.

GOING DEEPER

Parker Palmer's *Healing the Heart of Democracy: The Courage to Create a Politics Worthy of the Human Spirit* (2011) is a book for our times. At a point where the world seems to be more and more polarized around political and religious topics, Palmer humbly asserts that we should revisit President Lincoln's message in his second inaugural address. Palmer writes that "In his appeal to a deeply divided America, Lincoln points to an essential fact of our life together: if we are to survive and thrive, we must hold its divisions and contradictions with compassion, lest we lose our democracy" (p. 4).

I am a huge fan of Palmer's other works, and his wonderful book *The Courage to Teach: Exploring the Inner Landscape of a Teacher's Life, 10th Anniversary Edition* (2007) is my favorite gift for new teachers. Palmer writes beautifully about the importance of respecting others, living an authentic life, and the challenges and rewards of teaching. His other books are also definitely worth reading, and I learned about facilitating groups and life in general from his book *A Hidden Wholeness: The Journey Toward an Undivided Life* (2009).

Heidi Grant Halvorson's *No One Understands You and What to Do About It* (2015) is a accessible, evidence-based summary of research on communication. Grant Halvorson describes how what we think and do and what others think and do make simple communication difficult, and then describes strategies we can use to overcome those difficulties. Her book is especially useful for those whose work hinges on trust—as she gives excellent advice on how to build trust.

LOOKING BACK:

Finding Common Ground

Use this form to look at a conversation where you either did or did not find common ground.

Briefly describe the conversation you experienced.

_____

_____

_____

_____

What common denominators did you find between you and your conversation partner?

_____

_____

_____

_____

Please note any words that you or your conversation partner said that created unity or division during the conversation.

_____

_____

_____

_____

Did you do anything to avoid common dividers?

_____

_____

_____

_____

Is there anything you should do differently to be more effective at finding common ground?

_____

_____

_____

_____

LOOKING AT:

Finding Common Ground (1 of 2)

REGISTER

Keep track of interactions when you seek out common ground
for a day. What was the interaction? What did you do?
What was the outcome?

INTERACTION	WHAT DID YOU DO?	OUTCOME

Available for download at **http://resources.corwin.com/KnightBetterConversations**

LOOKING AT:

Finding Common Ground (2 of 2)

WITH A PARTNER

Use this form to explore Finding Common Ground and to try out the I-CARE model. Simply use the questions to identify what common ground you hold with your conversation partner.

Interests: What are your interests or passions (books, food, restaurants, music, sports teams, travel, and so on)?

....

....

....

Convictions: What are your important intellectual, political, artistic, social action, or religious beliefs?

....

....

....

Activities: What do you enjoy doing (cooking, running, singing, writing, volunteering, working, mentoring, and so on)?

....

....

....

Roles: What roles do you have or have you held (teacher, administrator, parent, committee member, scout leader, coach, choir director)?

....

....

....

Experiences: What are some important experiences you have had (schools or universities; people known; locations visited, lived in, or hope to be visited)?

....

....

....

....

LOOKING AHEAD:

Finding Common Ground

Who is someone with whom you want to find common ground?

....

....

....

Are you judging this person in any way that might make it difficult to find common ground?

....

....

....

What are some possible areas where common ground might exist or topics to avoid? Consider the acronym I-CARE.

....

....

....

I *Interests such as books, food, music, sports teams, local restaurants...*

C *Convictions such as intellectual, political, religious....*

A *Activities such as cooking, running, singing, writing....*

R *Roles such as teachers, administrator, parent, committee member, scout leader, choir director....*

E *Experiences such as schools or universities attended, people known, locations visited or hoped to be visited....*

What questions can you ask to find common ground?

....

....

....

....

Redirecting Toxic Words and Emotions

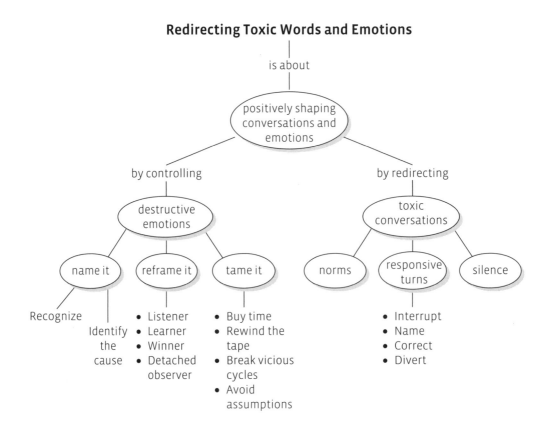

REDIRECTING TOXIC WORDS AND EMOTIONS

Our lives begin to end the day we become silent about things that matter.

—Martin Luther King Jr.

I have decided that there are too many people who enjoy hurting people with their words. I do not want to be in that camp.

—Research volunteer

Imagine yourself as the hero of an action thriller. Somehow, to save the day, you have to walk across a small plank that traverses a fiery lake filled with toxic waste. Every step you take, you keep your eyes on both sides of the board to make sure you maintain balance. You know one false step could dump you into the toxic mess, so you watch carefully and proceed with caution to ensure you get across the plank safely.

This is more or less what we need to do during emotionally charged conversations. We need to watch and keep in mind that a conversation could become toxic quickly, and when talk becomes toxic, we lose the chance to have a better conversation. When we interact, we need to make sure we don't fall into the toxic dump.

Consider two scenarios.

Scenario One: It is morning on a school day. The clock is ticking, and your son is still in the shower. He is going to be late for school, and you are likely going to be late for work. He is 16. He should get himself going without you having to tell him. It seems like he really doesn't care a bit if he's late, or more important to you, if you're late. You bang on the door and yell at him to get moving. Then, when he finally comes downstairs, you both run to the car without breakfast, and the drive to school is a long, silent, angry trip.

Scenario Two: Over a holiday meal at your in-laws, conversation circles around all the changes taking place in your spouse's home community. A visiting neighbor points out that the racial makeup of the town is changing, and to him the town just doesn't feel like home any more. Then he goes on to add, "Those people don't want us around anyway." An innocent conversation about their hometown has suddenly become a vehicle for racist comment. You are at your in-laws, and you don't want to cause trouble, but you heard what you heard. Remaining silent avoids conflict and speaking up might lead to angry comments at the friendly dinner table, but you have Martin Luther King's statement, "Our lives begin to end the day we become silent about things that matter," pinned to your bulletin board. What do you do?

In both scenarios, a conversation became toxic quickly. Little that is good comes out of hostile, demeaning conversations. Clearly, to have better conversations, we need to control our emotions so they don't poison our interactions, and we also need to speak up and shape conversations when other people's comments are damaging to others. This chapter describes how to deal with both kinds of toxicity.

Controlling Our Emotions

Some of the most toxic phenomena happen inside us. Our emotions, when getting the better of us, make it practically impossible for us to employ any of the Better Conversations Habits. When we are angry, we might not listen, interact, demonstrate empathy, or find common ground. In those moments, often all we want is revenge.

Participants in our study shared many situations where they had to work to control their emotions. Often their experiences occurred outside schools. As Susan Ellison wrote on her reflection form, and as many volunteers reported, "It is a lot easier to control destructive emotions at work than it is at home." Lisa Benham, for example, wrote about talking with her teenaged daughter about her F in English 12 during her senior year. By learning to control her emotions, Lisa wrote, she was able to shift from "being a frustrated Mom that can't understand why her daughter will not put forth the effort in her senior year!!" to being someone in control of her emotions. On her reflection form Lisa wrote:

> I've realized that allowing myself to consciously monitor my emotions has promoted my tolerance of events, people, and situations in which I usually am really frustrated. I have taken the power back to control destructive emotions that were draining my daily energy. This has especially helped me with my 18-year-old daughter, but also helped me promote goal-oriented topics in conversations with administrators.

Other volunteers described challenging situations where it was important for them to take the power back and control their emotions. Patty Brus wrote about regretting words she said at a funeral for a cousin, a marine who had died in combat. "Since the conversation," Patty wrote, "I have tried to reframe my emotions to respect individuals' choices and not impose my own." One research volunteer wrote about talking with her son about looking for a summer job and discovering how "paraphrasing my son's dialogue was a powerful tool in which potentially difficult emotions were avoided and meaningful conversations took place. Brilliant!!"

Our toxic emotions can negatively affect us in many ways. They can keep us from saying something that should be said, or they can prompt us to say something we will

I find that I am using this in all walks of life, not just in professional coaching. I am seeing aspects of my personal life differently because I am focusing on what I can do to control my reactions to situations. It is forcing me to think more about practicing what I preach.

—Ron Lalonde,
Middle School Principal, American School of Dubai

1. **Name It.** Identify situations where your buttons might be pushed and what the root cause is for your anger.

2. **Reframe It.** Change the way you think about emotionally difficult conversations by adopting a new frame for understanding them. See yourself as a listener, learner, game player, or a detached observer.

3. **Tame It.** Use one of the following strategies to keep your emotions under control: (a) buy time, (b) rewind the tape, (c) break vicious cycles, and (d) avoid making assumptions. Or, use your own strategies to maintain control of your emotions.

regret. "When we fail to control our destructive emotions," Debbie Kessler wrote, "we fail to hear what needs to be heard." For many reasons we need to control our emotions if we hope to have a better conversation. Three simple strategies can be used to do this—Name It, Reframe It, and Tame It.

The names for the three strategies—Name It, Reframe It, and Tame It—might seem kind of cutesy, but I have chosen these easy-to-remember names so when we are in the midst of emotionally charged interactions, we can easily recall them. As one research volunteer wrote, "The strategies are short and sweet and easy to think about," and LuAnn Fountaine wrote, "I think it is very helpful to have simple, concrete strategies to hold on to and to refer to often."

The three strategies are described in the box on the left.

NAME IT

The first way to control our emotions is to recognize when we are in a situation where we might react emotionally. If we can recognize a situation, topic, person, or other stimulus that might trigger an emotional response in us, we will be better able to maintain control of our emotions should we feel prodded or provoked. Sybil Evans and Sherry Suib Cohen, in *Hot Buttons* (2001), describe these triggers as hot buttons:

A hot button is an emotional trigger. Hot buttons get pushed when people call you names, don't respond to you, take what you think belongs to you, challenge your competence, don't respect you, give you unsolicited advice, don't appreciate you, are condescending. When someone pushes one of your hot buttons, it makes you a little crazy. That's all it takes. You explode. Not all explosions are loud, and maybe no one can see your eruptions, but you still explode inside. (pp. 1–2)

There are as many different hot buttons as there are people, and what triggers one person to jump out of his chair and shout may pass over another person like a cool summer breeze. Triggers can relate to our work, family, beliefs, or many other factors that are important in our lives. What matters, though, is that we recognize them before it is too late.

Many participants in our study wrote that being able to name potential triggers helped them plan for future conversations that might involve difficult emotions. Gretchen Brown, an instructional coach from Cecil County, Maryland, for example, wrote on her reflection form that she found it really helpful "to identify emotional situations before I enter into them. Being aware of these situations and preparing myself for them is more than half the battle."

An important but challenging part of "Naming It" is to try to identify the root cause of our anger. Organizational leaders often use a problem solving model known as Root Cause Analysis (RCA) to identify the true cause of a problem within an organization, and we can do something similar with our own emotions. The goal of RCA is to study a situation until you identify the real reason why a problem exists. You will know when you have gotten to a root cause when you recognize that removing the cause will resolve the problem.

RCA involves a variety of methodologies far more extensive than what is possible when we think about what makes us angry. A simpler strategy is one you may know that was first employed at Toyota Motor Company: The Five Whys.[1] We can use The Five Whys by stepping back and analyzing our situation until we identify the root cause of our anger. There is no magic in the number five. You might get to the root cause by asking fewer questions, or you might need to ask more questions.

Volunteers in our global study used The Five Whys to help them better understand their anger. One educational researcher wrote about a conflict when her sister told her to adopt their father's dog after their father was placed in a retirement home. The sister said she was allergic to dogs even though she had two of her own. The Five Whys helped the researcher realize that what really angered her was not the request, but that she allowed herself to be manipulated by her sister. She realized that if she could learn to resist that manipulation, she would stop being angry.

There are so many things working against us that I always just try to tell myself that nice matters. This doesn't mean I let myself be a pushover. I just take it as a personal challenge when I am frustrated to try to find the kindest way possible to resolve the problem. I find that this helps me when I feel my buttons being pushed because even if I am not understanding where someone is coming from, or someone is doing something that frustrates me, I still try to remember to be kind and respectful.

—**Stephanie Kilchenstein,** Instructional Coach, Cecil County, Maryland

---

[1]If you do a quick search online, you will find several descriptions of The Five Whys. The concept was largely popularized by Matthew May in *The Elegant Solution: Toyota's Formula for Mastering Innovation* (2007).

A principal of a school in China wrote about being upset because the district leader failed to acknowledge the work of his team and him. The Five Whys helped him see that he was angry because his team was underappreciated, but also because he felt he had failed to adequately advocate for his team. He realized that if he advocated more aggressively for his staff and was heard by district leaders, he would no longer feel angry.

The angry father described at the beginning of this chapter could also use The Five Whys. He might ask: Why am I angry? My son is making me late. Why does that make me angry? My son doesn't seem to care if he is late or if he makes me late. Why does that make me angry? He doesn't listen to what I say or care. Why does that make me angry? I feel like I could be doing a better job as a father. Why does that make me angry? I feel so overwhelmed with work that I can't do what I should, and I feel really guilty about that.

The Five Whys won't get the son out of the shower any faster, at least not at first, but the strategy could help the father see that his anger is more about him than about his son, and that realization could lead him to take a different approach. Maybe he will create a ritual that makes it possible for him to have more time and better conversations with his son. Perhaps he doesn't yet know what he will do, but he at least finds some comfort and control by understanding his emotions. Either way, once he names the root cause, the father at least has a chance to deal with his anger.

REFRAME IT

Often, naming the situation as one where our emotions can get the better of us is all we need to do to control our emotions—especially when we can identify a root cause. Also, when we identify a potentially emotionally complex situation in advance, we create a plan to go into the conversation prepared to keep our emotions under control. Unfortunately, though, there are often times, as Gretchen Brown wrote, when we "don't see the emotionally charged situations coming, and we find ourselves in difficult conversations before we realize it." In those moments, we need to learn how to reframe the interactions to better keep our destructive emotions under control.

We can understand the power of reframing if we imagine a simple scenario. Imagine you are driving your car and another car bolts through a stop sign, almost hits you, and then roars down the road. What would your reaction be? Odds are you might be tempted to engage in some angry, unpleasant nonverbal communication. But what if you knew that the driver of the car was a husband driving his pregnant wife to the hospital? Then you would only be concerned about the couple. You might even want to help them. Your anger would be gone.

Such is the power of reframing, and we can apply the method to help us control our emotions. To do this, we recognize and name a trigger when we see it, and then reframe the potentially negative situation so it becomes one we can control. Rather than allowing our emotions to have power over us, we "take back the power" by using reframing to stay in control. The reality of reframing is, as was the case with the husband rushing his wife to the hospital, sometimes our new frame is more accurate than our old one. When we reframe a conversation, we open ourselves to a better understanding, and we have a chance of keeping our emotions under control.

There are several ways you can reframe a potentially dangerous conversation to maintain control over your emotions.

Think of yourself as a listener. One simple way to reframe a conversation is to position yourself as a listener, and use the strategies of Habit 2, Listening With Empathy, to . . . well, listen. When you make it your task simply to take in everything your conversation partner says, you may keep yourself from saying things you will regret. Furthermore, if you make it a point to listen and really understand your conversation partners before you passionately tell them why you disagree, you may find that they actually agree with you.

Participants in our study shared what they learned when they reframed challenging conversations by thinking of themselves as listeners. Karen Taylor wrote on her reflection form, "Deciding to be the listener has made me a lot more cognizant of what the speaker is trying to say, so when I do say something, it's not reactive, and I have a better understanding of where the person is coming from." One participant wrote, "Listening is the key to controlling your emotions. Rephrase what the person is saying to show that you are listening. Wait to offer advice. Sometimes they just need to vent and then they will come up with answers that they are looking for."

Think of yourself as a learner. A second way to reframe an emotionally charged conversation is to think of yourself as a learner. In some ways, this is a focused way of seeing yourself as a listener. When you approach conversations as a learner, rather than reacting, you ask questions, listen, and dig deep to find out why the other person is as upset as she is. You reframe the conversation from one where you have to make your to point to one where you make it your point to identify the source of your conversation partners' emotion.

Andrea Broomell found herself in an emotionally charged conversation with her husband and decided to reframe her approach by thinking of herself as a learner. She and her husband were having a heated discussion about their daughter's behavior. When Andrea shifted to thinking of herself as a learner, she discovered that she and her husband actually had the same opinion. She wrote, "I realized that it was his agreement that was causing me to feel frustrated toward him! Poor fella!"

Have a personal victory. Another way to reframe a difficult conversation is to reframe it as a competition or game you win by maintaining control of your emotions. When people attack us or treat us badly, often what they want is for us to get angry, too. When we don't react, we throw the conversation out of balance, and keep our emotions under control. Stephanie Kilchenstein wrote, "I like the freedom of the 'Reframe step' because even when others are pushing your buttons, you can choose how to react, and we have control over that." She also wrote, "I continually try to keep in mind that others' perceptions are their reality, and I try to use that to help me keep perspective."

Go to the balcony. One of the world's leading experts on negotiation, William Ury, wrote about another strategy for controlling our emotions: going to the balcony. In *Getting Past No: Negotiating With Difficult People* (1991), Ury writes,

Going to the balcony means distancing yourself from your natural impulses and emotions . . . The balcony is a metaphor for a mental attitude of detachment. From the balcony you can calmly evaluate the conflict almost as if you were a third party. You can think constructively for both sides and look for a mutually satisfactory way to resolve the problem. (p. 38)

When I go to the balcony, as William Ury suggests, I literally imagine myself watching the conversation I'm involved in from above. This mental trick helps me feel detached from the emotion of the situation. As Jim Justice wrote, "Detaching myself from the emotion is key. The negative emotion totally hinders my ability to think rationally about stressful situations. I have to remember to be conscious of my intentions in the conversation and to behave in accordance to them."

In summary, a powerful way to maintain control of your emotions during tough conversations is to reframe the interaction and see it as an opportunity to (a) listen, (b) learn, (c) have a personal victory, or (d) detach.

TAME IT

Unfortunately, reframing the conversation may not be enough, so we need to have a repertoire of strategies to help keep our emotions under control. As a research volunteer wrote on her reflection form, "A conversation is not a conversation when emotions are out of control. Those interactions become like medieval jousts in which no matter who wins, everyone involved goes through unnecessary pain."

Some of the ways we can control our emotions are tricks our moms taught us, like counting to 10, and others are more complex. Many of them were first proposed by the outstanding thinkers at the Harvard Negotiation Project.

Buy time to think. According to William Ury (1991), "The simplest way to buy time to think in a tense negotiation is to pause and say nothing. It does you little good to respond when you're feeling angry" (p. 45). Simply counting to 10 slowly can work. Even taking a quick break from the conversation, say, to go to the restroom, can help. Ury suggests we "follow the biblical dictum: 'Be quick to hear, slow to speak, and slow to act'" (p. 46).

Katie Cook found "buying time" helped her "stop and think about different perspectives." She wrote, "Just giving myself more time to think and not respond so quickly made a difference." Another participant combined going to the balcony with buying time to think. She wrote, "I have learned to step outside the box and be an observer and to use wait time to put myself in the other person's shoes."

Part of buying time is choosing the right time to have an emotionally charged conversation. We should never make an important decision when we feel flooded with emotion. Deidre Smith wrote:

> I need to ensure that I do not attempt a difficult conversation when I'm already in a heightened state. I now believe it is better for me to postpone a potentially emotionally charged conversation until I am calm and have time to think and reflect. This will allow me to enter into the conversation and remain more aware of the potentially destructive emotions the topic might raise.

One of the easiest ways to buy time is to check in with our partners and make sure we understand what they said. To do this, we tell them everything we think we have heard them say. William Ury (1991) refers to this as rewinding the tape. He suggests we "slow down the conversation by playing it back. 'Let me just make sure I understand what you're saying'" (p. 46).

Others in our study found other ways to buy time. For example, one participant wrote that she "maintained eye contact and focused on my breathing to buy time to think about my reaction to the situation."

Break vicious cycles. Some conversations leave no room for graceful exits. When I am intent on proving you wrong, and you are intent on proving me wrong, we likely will find ourselves in a vicious cycle. As the following figure illustrates, the more aggressively I make my point, the more aggressively you will defend yours, and there is no easy exit.

Vicious Cycles in Conversations

Stone, Patton, Heen, and Fisher (2000) describe these vicious cycles as "what happened" conversations, in which "we spend much of our time . . . [struggling] . . . with our different stories about who's right, what meant what, who's to blame" (p. 9). If we recognize a vicious conversation cycle like this, the best we can do is stop the cycle by calling attention to it. Shawn Johnson from Cecil County, Maryland, used this tactic when he found himself leading a team that was headed toward a vicious cycle. Shawn headed off the conflict by saying, "It wasn't my intent for us to have this problem. Instead of getting more frustrated, let's work together to find a solution."

Don't make assumptions. One of the strategies I introduced in the chapter on dialogue, don't make assumptions, is also a powerful way to keep our emotions in check. Don Miguel Ruiz (2001) writes that

> The problem with making assumptions about what others are thinking is that we believe they are the truth. We could swear they are real. We make assumptions about what others are doing or thinking . . . then we blame them and react . . . We make

I like holding myself accountable. It is hard work, but worth the effort. This process allowed me to work myself through the process, analyze the situation, and change the direction because it was thought out and planned. I will ask for feedback to help my own growth and build the relationships at the same time.

—**Lisa Benham,**
Credential
Coordinator,
Fresno County
Office of Education,
Fresno, California

an assumption, we misunderstand, we take it personally, and we end up creating a big drama for nothing. (pp. 63–64)

Controlling our assumptions is easy to say and hard to do. Emily Peterson wrote that she found it challenging to keep her assumptions "in check," but when she did, she had to be "open to the very real possibility that I just might have something in common with someone I don't much care for!" She added, "It takes some real skill and effort for it to be genuine and sincere."

Our assumptions can lead us to be angry in situations where if we knew everything the other person was thinking, we might feel much more compassion than anger. For that reason, it is important to test out whether or not our assumptions are correct. To do that, the simplest way is to ask questions. Ruiz (2001), again, offers some suggestions:

Have the courage to ask questions until you are clear as you can be, and even then do not assume you know all there is to know about a given situation. Once you hear the answer, you will not have to make assumptions since you will know the truth. (p. 72)

In total, the three strategies that are a part of the habit of controlling toxic emotions—Name It, Reframe It, and Tame It—provide a set of strategies anyone can use to try to improve. No doubt, when it comes to implementing those strategies, many of us are like Stephanie Sandrock who wrote, "I am still very much a work in progress." To move forward, all we need is to start. And, to do that, we simply need to identify how we can get better and then do our best to implement the strategies that seem to work best for us. Juliana Dempsey wrote that during her reflection on conversations, she was able to create "containers" and identify exactly where her skills were breaking down. The coaching reflection forms have been designed to give everyone a similar opportunity to learn how they can have better conversations by maintaining control over their toxic emotions.

Use the *Looking Back: Controlling Toxic Emotions* form to analyze any potentially emotionally charged conversation from the past where you did or did not control your emotions. The form is meant to help you recognize what you did well and also areas where you might improve your ability to control your emotions.

Use the *Looking At: Controlling Toxic Emotions (1 of 2)* form to move through The Five Whys to identify the root cause for your anger. Keep asking yourself why until you identify what needs to be changed so you can extinguish your anger.

Use the *Looking At: Redirecting Toxic Emotions (2 of 2)* form to better understand how you physically react to prompts that make you feel strong, negative emotions. If you are a progressive in the United States, you might watch Fox News. If you are a conservative, you might watch MSNBC. Pay attention to how your body reacts. Does your skin feel extra warm, heartbeat quicken, or breath feel short? By understanding your emotions, you'll be better able to prepare for situations that might previously have surprised you.

Use the *Looking Ahead: Redirecting Toxic Emotions* form to plan how you can use the Name It, Reframe It, Tame It strategies to plan being in control during a conversation that has the potential to provoke you to react emotionally.

> Analyzing the situation I went through helped me take full responsibility for my role in creating drama. That was uncomfortable. I hope that I can think of all three categories next time I am in a similar situation—because I will be, because I have people in my life whom I care deeply about, because communication is difficult and takes an enormous amount of effort to do well in challenging situations.
>
> **—Research volunteer**

Redirecting Toxic Conversations

Controlling our emotions to avoid a toxic meltdown is one way to more frequently experience better conversations. However, creating a setting where better conversations can flourish also involves shaping the kind of conversations that happen around us. As Kegan and Lahey have written in *How the Way We Talk Can Change the Way We Work: Seven Languages for Transformation* (2001), a leader should be "a discourse-shaping language leader" (p. 20), standing against talk that is not respectful, open, and honest, while also remaining a part of the school culture. Everyone in a school can create a setting where better conversations will flourish by never giving toxic conversations a chance to begin.

The notion we should control conversations, even simply to root out hateful comments, might seem contradictory to the Better Conversations Belief that people should have a lot of autonomy; but autonomy in any civilization only extends so far. Autonomy cannot be used as a justification for language that dehumanizes others. We show respect not only by the way we communicate but also by the way we redirect others when they speak in dehumanizing ways. We do not redirect toxic conversations to close off dialogue or silence people with opinions different from our own. Our goal is to create an environment where better conversations flourish. To do this, sometimes we have to speak out in support of respect and correct others when they do not.

Correcting others is not easy, however. Amy is an instructional coach from the southern United States. She was confronted by a toxic conversation almost on her first day of work. When she was prompted to write about her experiences redirecting toxic conversations, Amy said she recognized that "I'm supposed to be a change agent, not an enabler of toxic conversations," but she admitted she struggled when she had to redirect conversations.

As a new coach in a new building, Amy was very keen to find ways to support teachers, and she scheduled one-to-one meetings with staff. In one of her first conversations, she felt lost as she listened to a teacher's toxic comments:

> As soon as the meeting started, the teacher was gossiping about other teachers in the building. We never had a chance to really get to the purpose of our meeting because for 30 minutes I listened to the teacher engage in toxic conversations.

"Very quickly," Amy wrote, "I recognized that the conversation needed to be redirected, but since this was my first year in a new building with new teachers, I went into panic mode. I wanted to be a good listener and build new relationships, but it felt as though I was only attentive to listen to his gossip." Amy added, "As I read the pages about toxic conversations, I realized that I feel worse today, almost a year later, than I did that day."

I wish I could report that toxic conversations like the one Amy experienced are rare, but every participant who wrote about toxic conversations was able to identify several examples. Many of the conversations dealt with gossip and criticism of others in the school, especially with respect to workload. Sadly, some were even more troubling. More

It is difficult. I feel preachy and better than thou when I try to stop toxic conversations. I know people are just blowing off steam and it is easy to convince myself that there's no harm in that. But I want people to see their conversations as a part of something larger. In the moment, the conversations never seem that important, but it is in the aggregate that the toxicity mounts.

—**Stacie Collins,**
English Teacher,
Northern Valley
Regional High
School, Old Tappon,
New Jersey

than half of the volunteers in the experiment reported being in conversations with people who made racist comments. Volunteers in the project had no difficulty finding toxic conversations to study.

A number of volunteers found themselves in toxic conversations with family members. One coach's comments describe the kind of situation many experience:

> I was with my husband's family prior to our marriage and there were very racially charged comments made. I was shocked and caught off guard, but due to the "newness" of my relationship with the extended family, I did not feel comfortable doing anything other than refuse to comment.

Every volunteer in the experiment recognized the importance of redirecting toxic conversations. For example, Stacie Collins wrote, "As a coach, redirecting toxic conversations is really important. The effectiveness of my position is dependent upon how trustworthy I am. If I engage in these types of conversations, how can anyone really trust me?"

Most volunteers, however, also mentioned how difficult it can be. One coach wrote, "I need to stay strong and recognize these toxic conversations from their outset. Then, I might be less tempted to get sucked in." Patty Sankey spoke for many who participated in the experiment when she wrote, "It is easy for me to redirect novice teachers, but I definitely struggle with people who are master teachers in the classroom, but toxic in professional settings."

Redirecting toxic conversations is a very important, complex task, and likely each situation is unique. Having said that, there are a few simple strategies that can help you keep toxic conversations from poisoning your organization's or your family's culture. Those strategies are (a) defining toxic conversations, (b) identifying your nonnegotiables, (c) stopping toxic comments before they start, (d) using responsive turns, and (e) silence. Each of the strategies is described below.

DEFINING TOXIC CONVERSATIONS

Toxic conversations are dehumanizing statements in which people are diminished, considered inferior, demeaned, or oppressed in some way. Thus, racist, sexist, homophobic

I think it's important to highlight the impact these conversations can have on the work of teachers and the culture of a school. As a middle school leader, I am not provided much training, although I am told that controlling toxic and difficult conversations is part of my role. To be effective at redirecting toxic conversations, we need an array of strategies, and we must also feel comfortable using those strategies properly. Having the leadership group look deeply at this topic would have a powerful effect—those conversations would be affirming and they would further build our capacity as leaders to continue tackling toxic conversations in a systematic and confident manner.

—**Alex Geddes,**
Middle School
Leader, Melbourne,
Australia

statements or conversations are obviously toxic. However, conversations that put people down or stereotype them are also toxic. We do not promote a safe and healthy emotional environment by engaging in gossip, abuse, or blame.

I find it useful to distinguish between what I call Level 1 and Level 2 toxic comments. Level 1 comments are rarely spoken in public, and they are obviously offensive. Racist, sexist, homophobic, and profane statements are Level 1 comments. A public figure would probably get fired for saying a Level 1 comment.

Unfortunately, as our global communication study shows, Level 1 toxic comments are often uttered in private. On vacations, in homes, and even during meetings in schools, the volunteers for this project reported, Level 1 comments are too frequently spoken. One teacher described how her colleagues attributed their students' success or lack of success to their race, and she wrote, "I realized immediately this was a toxic conversation by the way I was feeling about what was being said. It was disrespectful and stereotypical, and I was not comfortable sitting at the table." To her credit, she immediately redirected the conversation.

Level 2 comments are often more ambiguous, but nonetheless destructive. Gossip is a Level 2 comment; so is blaming others rather than accepting responsibility. Complaining and judging others can also be Level 2 toxic comments. Often Level 2 toxic comments are especially difficult to redirect. Stacie Collins wrote, "I don't encounter the overtly wrong (like racism, etc.) in my everyday dealings. It's the more subtle gossip that can seem innocuous enough but slowly poisons conversations."

The trouble with some Level 2 toxic comments is that people often feel pleasure when they hear something like gossip. As one coach wrote, "Hearing the gossip felt wrong from the get-go, but being included in gossip feels good." Don Miguel Ruiz describes this in *The Four Agreements* (1997):

> Gossiping has become the main form of communication in human society. It has become the way we feel close to each other, because it makes us feel better to see someone else feel as badly as we do. There is an old expression that says, "Misery likes company," and people who are suffering in hell don't want to be alone. (p. 38)

Gossip, Ruiz writes, is like a virus that infects a system or a poison that destroys a culture. Nothing good can be said of gossip. It diminishes the gossiper, breeds dishonesty, separates us from others, and all too often brings real pain to those who are its objects. Other Level 2 toxic comments are equally destructive. When people judgmentally blame others for their own struggles (teachers blame parents, coaches blame teachers, principals blame district leaders), they do damage by absolving themselves of responsibility and by making judgmental statements that belittle others' good intentions. To create an environment where better conversations can flourish, all educators need to adopt strategies that stop toxic comments from poisoning the environment.

STOP TOXIC CONVERSATIONS BEFORE THEY START

One way to redirect toxic conversations is to make sure they never happen. Leaders in organizations can accomplish this by establishing and reinforcing norms of respect and humanity. For norms to matter, everyone in a community has to have a voice in their development and agree that the norms are appropriate. Norms won't have much of an impact if they are written up and handed out as a done deal. People need to own them for them to work.

The norms also need to be enforced and reinforced. In part, that means leaders need to walk the talk, and it also means violations of the norms are identified and discouraged, preferably by everyone on the team.

When I was first studying instructional coaching, our team, guided by my colleague Mike Hock, established team norms. Everyone had a say in creating those norms, and we refined them until everyone felt proud of the statement we had created. Then, we used the norms as an evaluation tool for every meeting. Each of us would complete a survey online where we assessed how respectful, honest, and supportive we had been. Then, each meeting began with us reviewing the cumulative evaluations. In this way, we kept our norms present in our minds, and we each made adjustments when they were necessary to ensure our team was productive and positive.[2]

It is vital to redirect toxic conversations because when we let them progress, people say things that can't be taken back, and that affects the long-term working relationships. Toxic comments create bigger problems that are hard to resolve when people say things that don't respect the dignity of others affected by the conversation. But it is hard to redirect toxic conversations as they happen quickly, and the skill to recognize them and successfully choose an appropriate strategy takes thought and practice. It is easy to get caught in a toxic conversation when you can actually relate to the problem even if you wouldn't choose to deal with it in a toxic way.

—**Tess Koning,**
Lismore School District, New South Wales, Australia

---

[2] I've written more about how to establish norms in Chapter 6 of my book *Unmistakable Impact* (2011).

RESPONSIVE TURNS

When we redirect a conversation, the best approach is to address the words, not the person. If we judge others, we set ourselves up as superior, and as a result, we significantly limit our ability to ever engage in any kind of meaningful conversation with others in the future. To reject a person and leave no room for future conversation is a quick fix. We stop the words in the moment, but we never really address the more fundamental issue of what has been said.

In their book *The Shadow Negotiation: How Women Can Master the Hidden Agendas That Determine Bargaining Success* (2000), Deborah Kolb and Judith Williams suggest a strategy that can be used to redirect conversations—responsive turns. Kolb and Williams' book discusses negotiation, but their ideas of responsive turns can be applied to toxic conversations. Responsive turns are moves you can make to redirect a conversation. The authors suggest four moves: interrupting, naming, correcting, and diverting.

Interrupting. We can interrupt a conversation at any point if we feel we the need to stop. As Kolb and Williams (2000) write, "Interruptions stop the action. They prevent you from being swept up in a momentum that is not going your way" (p. 110). You can interrupt a conversation by taking a break or leaving the room (often because you recognize you are out of time). Kolb and Williams write that interruption is "such an important tool . . . [because] . . . it allows you time to regroup and consider what other responses you might have to make" (p. 113).

When Ruth Poage was leading a team discussion, she redirected the conversation by interrupting. "I didn't address what was said," Ruth wrote, "I just started another topic. I said something like, 'Let's get away from opinions and back to facts and things we can control.' Once we moved to facts and actions, things were productive. This is not to say, though, that beliefs were changed; they just were not tolerated at the table."

Naming. When we name what is happening in a conversation, we make the negative unspoken suggestions explicit. Kolb and Williams (2000) explain when using the naming strategy, you "let your counterpart know that you are perfectly aware of what is going on and are unfazed" (p. 109). Often, we can tactfully but clearly name another person's behavior by asking a simple question that pointedly states the negative implications of what has been suggested. "You don't really think that men should get paid more for doing the same job a woman does, do you?" Usually, when a toxic statement is surfaced, the speaker goes back on what he or she said.

Michelle Harris, an assistant principal in Beaverton, Oregon, wrote that she uses questions to name toxic comments. "I tend to get worked up about these kind of issues, so I think breathing and having some questions ready to go in my toolbox, so to speak, really helps," Michelle wrote. "I usually name what has been said by asking specific, open-ended questions." "It's getting easier the more I practice and do it," she said, "but I fail to redirect toxic conversations more times than I can count, and it is still hard, especially with family members."

Correcting. When we correct what has been said, we clarify that something communicated is simply incorrect. "Correcting turns," Kolb and Williams write, "go beyond simple protests and denials. They restore balance to the [conversation] by elaborating on just what's right about your rendering and why" (2000, p. 119). We can correct what has been said by making a statement, posing a question, or referring to an external source such as a trusted Internet website. Correcting "stop[s] moves the other person might use to justify holding you or your opinion in little regard" (p. 123). "I usually ask questions," Michelle wrote, "but sometimes if it is egregious, I have to make a statement."

Dehumanizing comments have to be stopped. We won't flourish in a society where hateful comments are allowed, but that doesn't make it easy. As Tess Koning wrote, "This is not an easy thing to do. You really need to understand adult learners and yourself. It takes a lot of practice to get comfortable redirecting conversations."

Diverting. We can divert conversations by simply taking them in a different direction. If we are talking with

Redirecting is a lot like asking the right questions as a coach. You want the teacher to reflect while you facilitate the conversation without saying too much. Less is more, so knowing the right question or the right strategies to redirect toxic conversations is essential.

—Tess Koning,
Instructional Coach,
Lismore School
District, New South
Wales, Australia

someone, and he or she wants to share some gossip, we can simply ignore the gossip and talk about something else. During a negotiation conversation, diverting the conversation usually turns the conversation away from a personal topic to a focus on the issues. More broadly, though, diverting simply redirects the conversation away from a toxic topic. Instead of gossiping about Tom, we divert the conversation and talk about Tom's daughter who just got a scholarship for an Ivy League university. That would probably be a better conversation anyway.

Tactics

Deborah Kolb and Judith Williams (2000) suggest that we can shape culture by redirecting conversations from unhealthy topics, like gossip, or other forms of destructive comments, by using communication maneuvers they call responsive turns. Responsive turns are communication tactics we can use to redirect potential unhealthy conversations. Four responsive turns suggested by Kolb and Williams, along with my definitions and some examples, are listed below:

Tactic	What Is It?	Example
Interrupt	Cutting off the negative conversation before it begins	"Oh crap, I'm late; I've gotta go."
Name	Describing what's going on so everyone can see it	"I just feel that if we keep complaining about kids, we're never going to come up with anything useful."
Correct	Clarifying a statement that is not true	"I was at the meeting, and Mr. Smith was actually opposed to the plan."
Divert	Moving the conversation in a different direction	"Speaking of Tom, when does the basketball season start this year?"

REMAINING SILENT

While staying silent may not seem like a powerful approach for stopping toxic conversations, strategic silence can be as clear a message as an explicit statement. When we are a part of a team, and the conversation takes a toxic turn, the best way forward may be simply to not participate in the discussion. Our refusal to participate—our silence—can speak volumes.

The attraction of some destructive conversations, like gossip, is that the persons who share their words with us make us feel like we are especially close, and that is why they share their information with us. "I wouldn't share this with just anyone," they might say, "but did you know . . . ?" However, the reality is we do not enhance any relationship by participating in a toxic topic. When we gossip, we show we are duplicitous and can't always be trusted. When we talk behind someone's back, our partner is right to ask, "What does he say about me when I am not around?"

Silence can be a clear way of indicating that we don't agree with gossip. Years ago I was on a team that spent far too much time criticizing others and gossiping. One member of the team, however, never once entered into the negative discussions. By staying silent, the team member communicated that she was a woman who could be trusted, and because of her silence, everyone on the team had a high opinion of her.

When we are confronted with a toxic comment, there are many responses we can take. If a racist comment is made at our in-laws' dinner table, we may choose to name the behavior by asking a question, "What is it that you experienced that leads you to say that?" or "You don't really think that every Latino in town is against you, do you?" Or you might choose to be silent, perhaps discussing the comment with your spouse later. What matters is that you identify the kind of conversations that are toxic, you develop the habit of always redirecting them in some way, and you practice until you can confidently stand up for conversations that communicate a deep respect for others.

> Developing the habit of redirecting toxic conversations is not only going to be a difficult task for me, but also for the people who are not used to this behavior in me. Often I resort to silence (something my mother told me to do). However, I have found that my silence doesn't stop the toxicity. I like having words and a plan to guide my conversations.
>
> **—Patty Sankey,**
> Sussex, Wisconsin

GETTING BETTER AT REDIRECTING TOXIC CONVERSATIONS

The first step in redirecting toxic comments is to identify the topics you believe should never be tolerated. For example, you might identify racist, sexist, or homophobic comments as always being unacceptable. You can use the *Looking Ahead* form to identify the kinds of conversations that are never acceptable and to identify the strategy you will use to redirect the toxic conversations. Following that, you can use the *Looking Back* form to analyze how effective you are at redirecting toxic comments.

The *Looking Back: Redirecting Toxic Conversations* form can be used to identify what you are doing well and how you can improve the way you redirect toxic conversations.

The *Looking At: Redirecting Toxic Conversations* form can be used to explore your beliefs about how you should react when you experience toxic conversations.

The *Looking Ahead: Redirecting Toxic Conversations* form can be used to identify the conversations you need to redirect and the strategies you will use to redirect them.

TO SUM UP

Better conversations will not occur if toxic emotions lead us to act in counter-productive ways, nor will they occur if toxic words or topics are allowed to take root. Fortunately, there are several strategies we can employ to control our emotions and redirect destructive comments.

We can control our emotions by using the following three strategies:

- **Naming:** Identifying situations where our buttons might be pushed and identifying the root cause for our destructive emotions.
- **Reframing:** Changing the way we think about emotionally difficult conversations by adopting a new frame for understanding them. Seeing ourselves as listeners, learners, winners, or detached observers.
- **Taming:** Using strategies to keep our emotions under control, including buying time, rewinding the tape, breaking vicious cycles, or avoiding making assumptions.

We can redirect toxic conversations by using a number of different strategies. Some of the most powerful are:

- **Establishing norms** with team members that can be reinforced and encouraged over time.
- **Using responsive turns,** especially those identified by Kolb and Williams (2000), which include interrupting, naming, correcting, and diverting.
- **Staying silent,** especially in situations where we feel our comments would not move us closer to a better conversation.

GOING DEEPER

Many books on the topic of negotiation have informed the development of the ideas in this chapter. In particular, the books from the Harvard Negotiation Project—especially Fisher, Ury, and Patton's *Getting to Yes* (1991); Ury's *Getting Past No* (1993); Stone, Patton, Heen, and Fisher's *Difficult Conversations* (2000); and Fisher and Shapiro's *Beyond Reason* (2005)—are all packed with valuable insight into the topics in this chapter. Roger Fisher and his colleagues have deeply influenced my thinking about interpersonal communication.

Deborah Kolb and Judith Williams' *The Shadow Negotiator: How Women Can Master the Hidden Agendas That Determine Bargaining Success* (2000) does not embody the partnership approach in the way that is evident in Roger Fisher's win-win negotiation, but the book provides excellent advice on how to turn a conversation away from a toxic topic.

Don Miguel Ruiz's *Four Agreements: A Toltec Wisdom Book* (1997) is a simple, wise book that many people treasure as one of the most important books they've read in their lives. Ruiz's four agreements are (a) Be Impeccable With Your Word, (b) Don't Take Anything Personally, (c) Don't Make Assumptions, and (d) Always Do Your Best. These are simple ideas, but, if they were embraced universally, they could have a profound, positive impact on our lives together.

LOOKING BACK:

Controlling Toxic Emotions

What was the topic of the conversation?

_____

_____

_____

Were you able to recognize that your hot buttons were going to be pushed?

○ Yes   ○ No

If no, what could you do differently in the future to recognize that what was happening was about to trigger an emotional response?

_____

_____

_____

Were you able to reframe the conversation so that you could maintain control of your emotions?

○ Yes   ○ No

If yes, what did you do? If no, what could you do differently in the future to reframe the conversation and maintain control of your emotions?

_____

_____

_____

What strategies did you use to maintain control of your emotions? Is there anything else you would like to try in the future?

_____

_____

What else could you try to do differently next time to maintain control of your emotions during difficult conversations?

_____

_____

_____

_____

LOOKING AT:

Controlling Toxic Emotions
(1 of 2)

ROOT CAUSE

Use this form to discover why something causes you to have destructive emotions.

Briefly describe an experience that made you angry.

....

....

....

....

....

Why did that make you angry?

....

....

Why did that make you angry?

....

....

Why did that make you angry?

....

....

Why did that make you angry?

....

....

Why did that make you angry?

....

....

What is the root cause for your anger?

....

....

....

....

LOOKING AT:

Controlling Toxic Emotions
(2 of 2)

MEDIA

Use this form to better understand your emotions. Identify some prompt that usually stirs destructive emotions. For example, if you are a progressive, you might choose to watch a very conservative television program, and if you are a conservative, you might choose to listen to very liberal media. While you are experiencing the prompt, pay attention to how your body reacts, what you think, and how you feel.*

What did you notice about how your body reacted? Did your skin feel extra warm, heartbeat quicken, or breath feel short? Did you notice anything else about how your body reacted?

What did you notice about how you were feeling? Did you feel angry, frustrated, confused, helpless, overwhelmed, sad, or some other emotion?

What else did you notice about how you reacted to the prompt?

If you watch this program while working out, you might get a much better workout than usual.

Available for download at **http://resources.corwin.com/KnightBetterConversations**

LOOKING AHEAD:

Controlling Toxic Emotions

Use this form to prepare yourself for a conversation that has the potential to provoke you to feel and act on destructive emotions.

How will you recognize that your emotions are being provoked (skin feels extra warm, heartbeat quickens, shortness of breath, unclear thinking, desire to respond without thinking, or something else)?

....

....

....

How will you reframe the conversation, if necessary (seeing yourself as a listener, learner, game player, detached observer, or in some other way)?

....

....

....

How can you use empathy to better understand others' perspectives, in particular their emotions and their needs?

....

....

....

What strategies can you use to tame your emotions to keep them under control (buy time, rewind the tape, break vicious cycles, equilibrate the conversation, avoid making assumptions, or something else)?

....

....

....

What else can you do to be prepared to control destructive emotions?

....

....

....

LOOKING BACK:

Redirecting Toxic Conversations

//.

Use this form to look at a conversation where you either did or did not redirect a toxic conversation.

Briefly describe the conversation you experienced.

....
....
....
....

How quickly did you recognize that this was a conversation you needed to redirect?

....
....
....
....

What did you do to redirect the conversation (interrupt, name it, divert it, or some other method)?

....
....
....
....

Were you satisfied with the outcome of the conversation?

....
....
....
....

Is there anything you should do differently to be more effective next time you encounter a difficult conversation?

....
....
....
....
....

LOOKING AT:

Redirecting Toxic Conversations

How important is it for you to redirect toxic conversations?

How easy is it for you to redirect toxic conversations?

Do you remember a time when you failed to redirect a conversation that was toxic?

If so, what was the conversation about?

What can you do in the future to be better at redirecting toxic conversations?

LOOKING AHEAD:

Redirecting Toxic Conversations

In the left-hand column below, list the kinds of conversations that you believe are never acceptable (racist, sexist, abusive, homophobic, gossiping, demeaning, blaming, or others).

Beside each topic, identify the strategy you will use to redirect the conversation (interrupt, name, correct, divert, or some other).

UNACCEPTABLE TOPICS	REDIRECTION STRATEGY

Available for download at **http://resources.corwin.com/KnightBetterConversations**

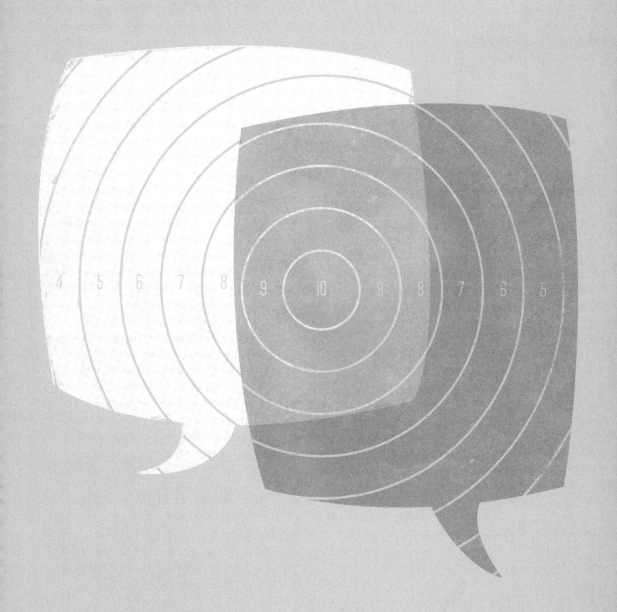

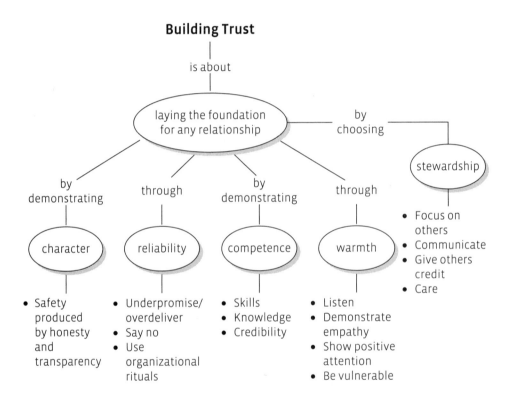

Building Trust

|
is about
|

laying the foundation
for any relationship

by
choosing

by
demonstrating

through

by
demonstrating

through

stewardship

- Focus on
  others
- Communicate
- Give others
  credit
- Care

character

reliability

competence

warmth

- Safety
  produced
  by honesty
  and
  transparency

- Underpromise/
  overdeliver
- Say no
- Use
  organizational
  rituals

- Skills
- Knowledge
- Credibility

- Listen
- Demonstrate
  empathy
- Show positive
  attention
- Be vulnerable

BUILDING TRUST

There is no way to lead schools successfully without building, establishing, and maintaining trust within and across the many and varied constituencies they serve. With trust, schools are much more likely to benefit from the collaborative and productive efforts of their faculty and staff, which in turn help generate the results for students that educators yearn for.

—Megan Tschannen-Moran (2014, pp. ix–x)

You cannot be an effective coach if you do not have the trust of the teachers. They need to see you as a person who supports them. My motto is "I am a teacher first and my job is to support and inspire teachers to be learners." I can't do that if I do not have their trust and respect.

—Candace Hall, Instructional
Coach, Richardson, Texas

For a few years now, I have written about the power of video to improve practice (Knight, 2014). My colleagues and I at the Kansas Coaching Project have field-tested the use of micro cameras, like iPhones, to improve teaching with instructional coaches from Beaverton, Oregon, and each of them tried out cameras with the teachers they coached.

When I tell audiences about the Beaverton coaches, they always ask one question: "How did they get teachers to agree to be video recorded?" People hearing about the coaches always worry that the teachers in their school will be hesitant to be filmed. So I asked the coaches, "How did you get teachers to agree to be recorded?" Their answer wasn't much help. "We just asked," the coaches said, "and the teachers agreed."

When we talked a little more, however, they were very helpful. "The reason the teachers agreed," they said, "is that they trusted us. When people refuse to be video recorded, the camera isn't the issue. The issue is trust. If people don't trust you, they won't want to be recorded." Then they added, "The reality is that if they don't trust you, not much coaching is going to happen anyway."

What the coaches told me was born out by what my colleagues and I found when we conducted what we called "The Great Coach Study." In 2009, eight researchers and I went to Florida to learn about the characteristics of outstanding coaches. We interviewed teachers, principals, coaches, and coaching supervisors in settings where coaches were having a big impact. One of our major findings was that the best coaching happens when teachers trust coaches. When there isn't trust, not much learning will happen.

Trust stands at the heart of so many of the good things that happen in schools. When teachers trust coaches, meaningful improvements can happen. When students trust teachers, real learning can happen, and when everyone trusts the principal, schools can be wonderful places to grow. Trust is also essential in our community, in our families, in our most personal relationships. When trust exists, there is learning, joy, and love. When trust does not exist, there is caution, inertia, and fear. Trust is just that important.

One of the first descriptions of trust that I encountered was the trust equation described by David Maister, Charles Green, and Robert Galford in their book *The Trusted Advisor* (2000). They suggest that trust can be expressed as a simple fraction:

$$\frac{\text{credibility, reliability, intimacy}}{\text{self-orientation}}$$

As with all fractions, the larger the numerator, the larger the number. Therefore, the more credible, reliable, and intimate we are with other people, the more people will trust us. The more we are focused on ourselves, however, the less people will trust us.

Credibility, the authors write, "isn't just content expertise. It's content expertise plus 'presence,' which refers to how we look, act, react, and talk about our content" (p. 71). We have to know our stuff, and others need to know that we know our stuff.

Reliability, the authors write, "is about whether clients think you are dependable and can be trusted to behave in consistent ways . . . Reliability is the repeated experience of links between promises and action" (p. 75). When we are reliable, we do what we say we are going to do, and we don't make promises we can't keep.

Intimacy, the authors write, "is about emotional closeness . . . People trust those with whom they are willing to talk about difficult agendas (intimacy), and those who demonstrate that they care (low self-orientation)" (p. 77). Intimacy may be a slightly distracting term since it has so many different connotations, but the authors' point is that when we are intimate with people, we share our lives with them, and they share their lives with us. The less we hold back, the more trust there will be.

"There is no greater source of distrust," according to Maister, Green, and Galford (2000), "than advisors who appear to be more interested in themselves than in trying to be of service to clients" (p. 80). They add, "Self-orientation is about much more than greed. It covers any thing that keeps us focused on ourselves rather than on our client" (p. 80). If our interactions are all about me, there is a very good chance you won't trust me.

Many others have offered frameworks for understanding trust. Megan Tschannen-Moran in *Trust Matters: Leadership for Successful Schools* (2014) identifies five facets of trust: (a) benevolence, "the confidence that one's well-being or something one cares about will not be harmed by the person in whom one has placed one's trust" (pp. 21–22); (b) honesty, the belief that "the statements [someone] makes are truthful and conform to 'what really happened'" (p. 25); (c) openness, the "process by which people make themselves vulnerable to others by sharing information, influence, and control" (p. 28); (d) reliability, "the sense that one can depend on another consistently"

(p. 33); and (e) competence, "the ability to perform a task as expected, according to appropriate standards" (p. 35).

Stephen R. Covey, in *The Speed of Trust: The One Thing That Changes Everything* (2006), identifies 13 behaviors that he sees as essential for building trust. Although the list is lengthy (13 behaviors long!), a lot can be learned by looking over all the behaviors, so I have included all of them below.

1. Talk straight, which "is honesty in action . . . it means two things: to tell the truth and leave the right impression" (p. 137).

2. Demonstrate respect, which involves two critical dimensions, "first to show fundamental respect for people, and second, to behave in ways that demonstrate caring and concern" (p. 145).

3. Create transparency, which "is about being open. It's about being real and genuine and telling the truth in a way that people can verify" (p. 153).

4. Right wrongs "is more than simply apologizing; it's about making restitution. It's making up and making whole. It's taking action. It's doing what you can to correct the mistake" (p. 159).

5. Show loyalty involves "two dimensions: giving credit to others, and speaking about people as though they were present" (p. 166).

6. Deliver results is accomplished when people "establish a track record of results. Get the right things done. Make things happen. Accomplish what [they were] hired to do. [Are] on time and within budget. Don't overpromise and underdeliver. Don't make excuses for not delivering" (p. 176).

7. Get better "is based on the principles of continuous improvement, learning and change . . . When people see you as a learning, growing, renewing person . . . they develop confidence in your ability to succeed" (p. 178).

8. Confront reality "is about taking the tough issues head-on. It's about sharing the bad news as well as the good, naming the 'elephant in the room,'

addressing the 'sacred cows,' and discussing the 'undiscussables'" (p. 184).

9. Clarify expectations "is to create shared vision and agreement about what is to be done upfront" (p. 193).

10. Practice accountability has two key dimensions. "The first is to hold yourself accountable; the second is to hold others accountable" (p. 200).

11. Listen first, which "means not only to really listen (to genuinely seek to understand another person's thoughts, feelings, experience, and point of view), but to do it first (before you try to diagnose, influence, or prescribe)" (p. 208).

12. Keep commitments is "the Big Kahuna" of all behaviors. It's the quickest way to build trust in any relationship . . . [and] its opposite—to break commitments or violate promises—is, without question, the quickest way to destroy trust . . . when you make a commitment, you build hope; when you keep it, you build trust" (p. 215).

13. Extend trust "is different in kind from the rest of the behaviors. It's about shifting from 'trust' as a noun to 'trust' as a verb . . . It creates reciprocity; when you trust people, other people tend to trust you in return" (p. 223).

In *No One Understands You and What to Do About It* (2015), Heidi Grant Halvorson offers another perspective on trust. She explains, first, that the root of our experience of trust

> lies in humans' distant past, when determining whether another creature meant you harm was priority number one, all day, every day. In the modern era we worry less about our physical safety (though we do still worry about that, too) and more about whether new acquaintances are trustworthy. (p. 66)

For that reason, Halvorson writes, people are interested in basic concerns when they consider whether or not they can trust someone. Halvorson writes, "Studies suggest that in order to figure out whether you are trustworthy, others analyze your words and deeds to find the answer to two questions:

1. Do you have good intentions toward me—are you a friend or foe?

2. Do you have what it takes to act on those intentions? (p. 67).

I got another perspective on trust by asking the participants in our global communication study to reflect on books, television shows, or movies and identify the characteristics of characters who were trustworthy and those who were not. The volunteers did not disappoint. They wrote about watching such varied movies or shows as *The West Wing*, *Momma Mia*, *The Mistresses*, *Psych*, *FX*, *Austin & Ally*, and *Lost*. Others considered books like *The Shack* and *To Kill a Mockingbird*. Each volunteer completed the *Looking At: Building Trust* form, which is included at the end of this chapter. A summary of what they wrote is presented in the following table. You and your colleagues can also analyze trust by filling out the form.

Trustworthy Traits	Untrustworthy Traits
• Loyal	• Disloyal
• Able to admit when wrong	• Unable to admit when wrong
• Owns their own stuff; responsible	• Blames; cannot own their stuff, irresponsible
• Tells the truth, even at personal cost	• Hides the truth, lies
• Others-focused	• Self-focused and self-pitying
• Open-minded	• Closed-minded
• Good listener	• Doesn't listen well
• Habitually compassionate	• Lacks compassion
• Shows integrity; leads by example	• Lacks integrity, both verbally and physically
• Kind	• Kind in order to get something; otherwise generally unkind
• Honest, genuine, transparent	• Dishonest, ingenuous, sly, sneaky
• Refuses to manipulate	• Manipulative
• Doesn't gossip	• Gossips
• Giver, generous without strings attached	• Taker
• Respectful of others	• Bossy

Trustworthy Traits	Untrustworthy Traits
• Focused on solutions	• Focused on problems
• Doesn't whine	• Whines
• Nonjudgmental	• Judgmental
• Has lots of good, long-term friendships	• Lacks good, long-term friendships
• Fair-minded, transparent	• Cheater
• Isn't afraid to be vulnerable	• Never shows vulnerability
• Avoids being late	• Careless of others' time
• Puts forth clear, solid effort	• Puts forth minimal effort
• Doesn't seek glory	• Seeks glory
• Takes self lightly	• Cannot laugh at oneself
• Uses anger appropriately	• Gives full vent to anger
• Displays an open, guileless face	• Displays a closed demeanor
• Empathetic	• Lacks empathy
• Protective of others' dignity and person	• Does not care about protecting others' dignity and person
• Encourages	• Discourages
• Gracious, without agenda	• Ungracious—unless they want something or are covering up
• Has no hidden agenda	• Has a hidden agenda
• Allowing for others' choice	• Controlling
• Reliable	• Unreliable
• Preserves the dignity of another person	• Makes fun at others' expense
• Speaks appropriately, isn't the loudest person in the conversation	• Talks too much, too loudly
• Willing to admit when wrong	• Unwilling to admit when wrong
• Displays integrity of speech	• Duplicitous
• Has their stuff together	• Slick
• Makes sure people are aware	• Enjoys surprising people and putting them on the spot
• Doesn't play games	• Player
• Is frank without being harsh, tactful, gracious	• Harsh, tactless, graceless
• Speaks with clarity	• Speaks vaguely
• Engages others	• Engages others to get their way

Trust is vitally important. Halvorson's review of the literature leads her to conclude that "the benefits of projecting trustworthiness (and the costs of failing to do so) are enormous" (p. 66), and Tschanen-Moran stated in an interview for "in conversation," a publication of the Ontario Department of Education, that trust "is one of the few variables that educational researchers have found that outstrips socioeconomic status as a predictor of student achievement" (p. 7). At the same time, trust is both a very complicated concept and a very simple one. It is complex because as the various authors cited above show, trust can be described in many ways. But it is also very simple because usually when we hear others say, "I just don't trust him," we have a very clear understanding of what they mean.

Trust Factors

Based on a review of the literature, my experience working with educators from six continents, and feedback from the volunteers in our study, I have identified five trust factors: character, competence, reliability, warmth, and stewardship. Each of these characteristics is described below.

CHARACTER

If we want to be trusted, we need to be people of character, who live in ways that others consider ethical. If you act in untrustworthy ways, you can't expect others to trust you. This may seem obvious, but it must be stated. If you lie or cheat, you will eventually be caught, and when you get caught, trust will be destroyed, sometimes so profoundly that you will never regain it. The first part of building trust is to simply be an ethical person.

The reason why honesty and ethical behavior are so important for building trust is, as Heidi Grant Halvorson has written, that one of our first thoughts when we consider whether we should trust someone is whether or not they have our best interests at heart. Halvorson writes, "We want to know if other people pose a threat to us—to our relationships, to our careers, to our overall happiness and well-being. Are you going to make trouble for me? We wonder" (p. 66). As one of the participants put it a bit more directly, "I want to know whether or not they are going to screw me over."

We trust people when we know they want us to succeed, and when they mean us no harm. In *Integrity: The Courage to Meet the Demands of Reality* (2006), Henry Cloud describes the kind of person that most of us would consider trustworthy:

> True trust comes when we realize that another's goodness, and being for my best interest, is not dependent on anything. It is just a part of that person's integrity. It is who that person is, the kind of person who wants the best for others and will do whatever he or she can to bring that about. Then, there is nothing to fear. If I mess up, you will be there for me. (p. 83)

Honesty is critical for trust because once I realize you are dishonest, I can never be safe with you. Also, when people choose to be dishonest, almost always they are choosing something better for themselves than for others. People lie to get something that they might not get if they are open. Participants in our study saw honesty as a critical part of building trust. One instructional coach spoke for many participants when she said, "One of the things I pride myself on more than anything else is my honesty. It is not always pretty, but it is the truth. People may not like what is said, but they appreciate that it came from a place that was not malicious or fluffed up. There is nothing like being told you are amazing only to find out you are average."

Dishonesty, of course, has many faces. Little white lies are lies just the same. Flattery is a form of dishonesty (again, often done to get something from someone). Withholding information is a form of dishonesty. Gossip, too, is a form of dishonesty. When people gossip, their actions show that what they say in front of one person is different than what they would say in front of others. Gossips are duplicitous, which is to say, untrustworthy, and as instructional coach Sarah Aguilar wrote, "I do not trust someone that I hear all the latest gossip from."

One way to demonstrate character is by being transparent. Megan Tschannen-Moran (2014) writes that openness, her term for transparency, "means the disclosure of facts,

> One of my strengths is my honesty and trustworthiness. It has taken 13 moves, a divorce, a child, a new marriage and two deaths in my family over the last few years to make me really reevaluate myself. It has been those obstacles that I have overcome that have helped me empathize with others in a nonjudgmental and honest way. I don't willingly offer up my past, but when speaking to others in hard conversations, it is then that they truly see that I am coming from a place of honesty and with that builds trust.
>
> —**Sarah Pankonien,**
> Instructional Coach,
> Richardson, Texas

The only thing you have is your reputation. Make it count.

—**Sarah Aguilar,**
Instructional Coach,
Kenosha, Wisconsin

alternatives, intentions, judgments, and feelings" (p. 29). As Carol McBroom wrote on her reflection form, "I don't want people to wonder what I am really thinking or what hidden agendas I might have. I want our conversation to be one where both of us feel comfortable and feel our thoughts are heard." Transparency, Henry Cloud (2006) writes, is a characteristic of effective leaders that has two aspects.

> They are transparent in that they let the reality of where they are and the situations be known. We can only ultimately trust people who are being real with us. But part of that is transparency not just about the facts, but about themselves as well. We need to see their vulnerabilities, and how they are feeling about things. We also need to know about their failures, and times when they haven't gotten it right. That helps us to follow them. (p. 95)

If we withhold information from others, they will be reticent to put their faith in us, likely wondering what it is that we are holding back. To engender trust, we need to do our best to be as transparent as we can. In some situations, we will certainly need to keep information private, such as if we are on a hiring committee. In general, however, the more open we are, the more people will trust us.

Other aspects of character build trust, but many of those are described in the other characteristics in this chapter. Not the least of these is reliability.

RELIABILITY

Reliability is also an essential characteristic of trustworthiness. Whatever our role, if we want people to trust us, we must be careful to deliver what we say we will deliver, to meet when we say we will meet, and to keep our promises. Sarah Aguilar described it this way. "Reliability is crucial. *If* you say you will be there, be there. It takes a lot for a teacher to share control of the classroom and, if you have gotten your foot in the door, do what you can to keep the door from shutting."

Maister, Green, and Galford (2000), who identify reliability as one the three critical positive factors for building trust, write that reliability "is about whether clients think you are dependable and can be trusted to behave in consistent ways . . . it has an explicit action orientation. It links words and deeds, intention and action" (p. 74). Tschannen-Moran (2014) describes how important reliability is in schools:

> The sense that one can depend on another consistently is an important element of trust. Teachers may conclude that their principal is a nice person and means well, and even that he or she is very capable and helpful if they can get his or her attention. But if overcommitment, trouble managing the time demands of the job, or being easily distracted means teachers cannot count on the principal to come through for them when needed, trust will not characterize the relationship. (p. 33)

One way to increase reliability is to be careful not to promise too much. For many educators, the temptation is to agree to anything in the hopes of moving school improvement along. Although well intended, this is a potentially dangerous practice. Making a promise and not delivering on time can be much more damaging to a relationship than explaining that it may take a week or two before you can provide whatever is needed. A better practice is to under-promise and overdeliver.

One of the main reasons we struggle to be reliable is that we take on too many tasks for the time that we have. We can be so busy doing everything that we end up doing very few things well. Many of the volunteers in our study reported that their experiences were similar to what Sarah Pankonien wrote on her reflection form:

> Last year I tried to do it all—specialist, classroom teacher, assessment team member, etc. I was stretched to the gills. I was becoming a jack-of-all-trades, but a master of none. This year I have had to take a few things off my plate. My focus on instruction and teachers on the campus will be my first priority. I owe it to our students, fellow teachers, and myself to be focused and on task.

To find the time to be reliable, we need to be intentional about how we use our time. For most people, this does not

> It's better to be super reliable to a few than semi-reliable to many.
>
> **—Lindsey Meyers,**
> Instructional Coach,
> Richardson, Texas

mean that we need to buy a new planner or app and "manage our days better." Most people look at their calendars and simply don't see any free time to do what they want to do. To be more reliable, we need to find more time, by either cutting out parts of what we do—resigning from committees or other activities that take a lot of time—or establishing boundaries—for example, coaches might limit the number of teachers they work with in a week.

Another way to become more reliable is to adopt organizing rituals—little routines you build into your life to help you be more reliable. For example, a principal might set aside time at the start of each day to identify the most important tasks she must implement that day. Similarly, a teacher might review the list of her students at the end of each week to consider what she needs to do to encourage or support each student's learning.

Carol Fancher wrote that she had to use a lot of tools to ensure that she was reliable. She wrote, "In order to do my job well, I've had to learn organizational techniques—and become the master of my Google calendar with reminders all day long for important things, as well as simple tasks." People want to know that they can count on you to do what you said you would do. However, they also want you to deliver on your promises. To do that, you have to have the skills necessary to help people (children or teachers) to meet their goals. And for that to happen, you have to be competent.

COMPETENCE

One of the factors that increases trust is competence. We trust people who know what they are talking about and who deliver on what they promise. Students will be more inclined to trust teachers who provide the instruction and feedback they need to succeed. Teachers are more inclined to trust instructional coaches, for example, when those coaches can help them meet their goals and reach more students. Principals who want to have helpful conversations with teachers around an instructional framework need to have a deep understanding of that framework. Heidi Grant Halvorson (2015) explains that warmth (described later in this chapter) and competence are both essential for trust:

I recently moved into a new office on campus, and as I unpacked, I hung up a poster with the quote by Eleanor Roosevelt, "Great minds discuss ideas; average minds discuss events; small minds discuss people." This is to serve as a constant reminder to myself to think about what I say as well as the conversations in which I participate. I don't ever want to alienate others by displaying a lack of character or reliability.

—Alison Duty,
Instructional Coach,
Richardson, Texas

Decades of research show that [people] are highly tuned into two particular aspects of your character, right from the get-go—your warmth and your competence. Your warmth—friendliness, loyalty, empathy—is taken as evidence that you have good intentions toward the perceiver. Your competence—intelligence, skill, effectiveness—is taken as evidence that you can act on your intentions if you want to. Competent people are therefore valuable allies or potent enemies. Less competent people are objects of compassion or scorn—if we bother to think about them at all. (pp. 66–67)

Megan Tschannen-Moran found the same thing and cites other studies that support her findings. "Goodwill and good intentions are not always enough to garner the trust of others. When a person is dependent on the skills and abilities or another, even an individual who means well may not be trusted" (2014, p. 35).

Competence is different for different professions. Competent instructional coaches have a deep knowledge of the teaching strategies they share, and they can describe them precisely, perhaps through the use of checklists. They need to go deep in their learning of the practices they share, reading manuals, books, and articles over and over and developing and refining checklists that describe what they do. Teachers understand and use effective teaching strategies, and they know the impact of those strategies. Administrators have a deep understanding of the tools they use and share. If they are using a framework for assessing teaching, for example, they need to know with certainty that their observations are reliable. If their school is implementing a reading program, they need to know that program inside out.

To improve, educators should use coaches, video, and other supports to master the skills and knowledge they need to gain the trust of parents, students, and their colleagues. Many of the volunteers in our study were able to pinpoint areas where they needed to improve to be more competent. One instructional coach wrote, for example, "I learned that there is one aspect of building trust that I need to get better at, and that has to do with increasing my math pedagogical knowledge. I have been a coach for one year, and I still have a long way to go."

Part of competence is communicating that you are competent. In my experience, the most important way to do that is to move forward respectfully and with confidence. If we constantly call attention to what we don't know, our lack of knowledge will be what people notice. I don't think we should be deceptive, ever, and we shouldn't say we know what we don't know, but we shouldn't be overly tentative.

Imagine for a second a gifted young pianist who stops and says oops every time she makes a mistake. A better strategy for her is to play through the mistakes without calling attention to them. Most of us won't notice the few mistakes that are made, and we'll enjoy the performance so much more. In the same way, I think we can communicate confidence by playing through our few mistakes and moving forward.

Heidi Grant Halvorson (2015) gives many suggestions on ways we can communicate competence. We should make eye contact. We should demonstrate that we have will power. We should balance out communicating our experience and skills with humility. We should never be defensive. No doubt those strategies help us look competent, but I think the best strategy is to use all the supports we have to get good at what we do. To really look like we're competent, we need to be competent.

Finally, an important part of competence is to be credible. One important way that principals, coaches, staff developers, and educational researchers can stay credible is by spending time teaching lessons that employ the teaching strategies they share. This most frequently involves co-teaching or modeling lessons. The closer leaders are to the classroom, the more competent and credible they will be.

Another way to be credible and competent is for leaders to walk the talk. If principals think teachers should be using video to improve their practice, the principals should be doing that. If teachers want students to hand in assignments promptly, they should return assignments promptly. Our credibility is demonstrated by knowing what it is like to be in others' shoes. When we clearly understand others' perspectives, we'll have more credibility. If people see us as credible, they'll be more likely to trust us.

Competence to me means putting your money where your mouth is. Be ready to do what you ask of your colleagues, and know how to show what you are talking about. Talk and no action will not lead to a successful coaching relationship, and trust will definitely not be built.

—**Sarah Aguilar,**
Instructional Coach,
Kenosha, Wisconsin

WARMTH

We trust people when we feel safe with them and when they don't threaten us. So, it follows that we are more inclined to trust people who are nice. A snarly man or woman who intimidates us is not likely a person who will inspire trust. This is important because we usually are not aware when we are deciding whether or not we trust someone. Halvorson (2015) writes,

> The decision to trust is made almost entirely unconsciously and is based on the extent to which you project warmth and competence. Warmth is a signal that you have good intentions toward your perceiver; competence signals that you are capable of acting on those intentions. (p. 84)

We know we can trust someone when they have our best interests at heart—that is, that they genuinely care about our well-being. Many of the habits and beliefs in this book, if taken to heart and lived out, will demonstrate that we really do care. When we listen and demonstrate empathy, when we really want to hear what others have to say, we show that we care. When volunteers in our study described people they trusted, often they mentioned that the person they trusted listened to them and cared. Sarah Pankonien, for example, wrote the following:

> Someone that I trusted implicitly was my grandmother. She was someone that I could tell anything to and she would first listen—then relate. It always made me feel as if she had been in my shoes, even if she hadn't been, and she validated my concerns. Her empathy and love was unconditional, and she always made time for me.

Validation, a trait that Pankonien mentions above, is another way people can demonstrate warmth. We trust people when they see the good in us, and especially when they see good that we can't see. We validate others by communicating that we have faith that they are good people and that they are valuable.

A person I trust is Dave Cawthorn—my father—I know that he always wanted what was best for me and all others he met. He was a man of his word and meant what he said. He was not afraid to have hard conversations that are a requirement of trust, but he always spoke in a caring manner. Most importantly, his interactions with others showed a positive pre-supposition for those he dealt with. This enabled him to focus on their strengths and resulted in positive interactions.

—**Carol McBroom,**
Instructional Coach,
Richardson, Texas

I think warmth goes beyond being an effective communicator and being trustworthy. Like an effective teacher in a classroom who takes an interest in his or her students' lives outside the classroom, coaches can show warmth by simply asking about a teacher's weekend, how their birthday party went, how their child/children are doing, etc. This demonstrates warmth, compassion, to a teacher and goes a long way in helping to develop trust.

—Craig Wisniewski,
Instructional
Coach, Newington
Public Schools,
Connecticut

The opposite of validation is judgment, which I have discussed in many parts of this book. Many of the volunteers on this study reported that they knew they had to stop being judgmental. The problem is that when we judge people, we cut off any chance for intimacy, and decrease the chance that people will trust us, because judgment sets us up as better than the person we judge. This is not to say that we shouldn't gather data or evaluate, but judgment is when we observe and then directly or indirectly make a negative statement about someone's character or competence.

The Habit of Being a Witness to the Good is a powerful way to validate others. This is not to say that we hide from the truth, but just to say that when we notice something is going well, we mention it in a nonjudgmental way. Being a witness to the good is usually positive for the giver of the good news as well. Lou Sangdahl writes that "Witnessing the good is fun, and I love sharing or posting the great things I see people doing." Similarly, Candace Hall writes, "Relationships are works in progress, a bit like a roller coaster. You celebrate the positives and negatives. It's a vital part of an instructional coach's job."

A final way people demonstrate warmth is through vulnerability. Many of the volunteers stated, as Candace Hall wrote on her reflection form, "No one is perfect, and relationships are hard work and you have to be vulnerable sometimes." By being vulnerable, we make ourselves approachable and we show that we are like others. Vulnerability creates intimacy, one of the factors that Maister, Green, and Galford (2000) identified as essential for trust. Intimacy, they write, "is driven by emotional honesty, a willingness to expand the bounds of acceptable topics, while maintaining mutual respect and by respecting boundaries" (p. 77).

STEWARDSHIP

When we adopt a stewardship approach, we foster trust by putting others' interests ahead of our own. I was introduced to the concept of stewardship in Peter Block's *Stewardship: Choosing Service Over Self-Interest* (1993). In this book, stewardship has many meanings, but among them is the notion that "stewardship is to hold something in trust for another . . . [choosing] service over self-interest most powerfully when we build the capacity of the next generation to govern themselves" (p. xx). "The underlying value" of stewardship, Block writes, is about "deepening our commitment to service" (p. xx).

In large part, we can demonstrate stewardship simply by not being self-focused. For this reason, we must ensure that conversations are not "all about me" but all about everyone in the conversation. We need to listen much more than we talk and monitor our thinking and conversation so we don't let our ideas dominate. Taking the time to truly listen is one of the most respectful things we can do.

Moving away from a self-focus also ensures that our actions and concerns are about others and not ourselves. Thus, coaches, for example, should take every opportunity they can to give credit to others when there are successes, or in a similar fashion, take the blame rather than letting others be blamed. One participant in our study wrote about how she felt when she was given credit: "Giving credit resonated with me. I've noticed that my new school's administrative team members give me credit and thank me both publicly and privately. I feel valued and energized when others tell me that my contributions matter."

Additionally, we should genuinely express concern for students, teachers, administrators, and others in the school because it's not "all about me"; it is all about the kids. Effective educators recognize the moral purpose inherent in the work they do, and they are driven by a desire to see their students grow, their school improve, and their students achieve. When we see stewardship in others, we are much more likely to trust them.

We demonstrate stewardship by genuinely expressing concern for students, teachers, and administrators. More than anything else, when we take a stewardship approach, we genuinely put others' self-interests ahead of our own, or we at least see theirs as being as important as our own. Carol Fancher summed this up beautifully when she described the work she does as an instructional coach in Richardson, Texas:

I love my job and my school—because of our faculty. We are very close-knit. I discovered years ago that teachers often need a shoulder to cry on or someone they can vent to. They know my door is always open and they're always welcome. Sometimes being vulnerable or personally transparent is hard for me—but I've had several family struggles that I felt I couldn't pretend weren't happening, and when I was open about them, I was the receiver of warmth and support. We're all vulnerable.

—**Carol Fancher,**
Instructional Coach,
Richardson, Texas

I truly admire our teachers and the magic they perform. The first year I was instructional specialist, I was able to be in many of their classrooms—and was amazed at all the wonderful teaching going on. I made it my mission to get the word out to teachers and administrators so that we could learn from one another. My role is to support—and I have never desired to be in the spotlight. It's just not my personality. I get the most pleasure from being able to help others.

Trust: Putting It All Together

Better conversations are difficult without trust. When people in conversations trust each other, they share their thoughts openly without fear. When people don't trust each other, their conversations can be cautious, empty, even frustrating and dehumanizing. As I've heard more than one person say, trust is like the air we breathe. We don't notice when it is there, but when it is gone, everything stops.

One of the most powerful ways to build trust is to adopt and apply the Better Conversations Beliefs and Habits. If we believe in equality, autonomy, nonjudgmentalism, and that other people all deserve to be heard, we will build more trust. And when we listen, find common ground, build connections, redirect our toxic emotions, and demonstrate empathy, we also build trust. Each habit or belief reinforces the others. Empathy helps us be better listeners, and when we listen we connect and discover what we hold in common with others.

These are not small changes to make. To become a better listener, just to take one example, can require a lot of planning and practice. But we can get better. The experiences reported by many of our volunteers demonstrate that, and your experiences can prove it to you.

Getting better at conversation is extremely important work. When our conversations improve, we improve at work, in our community, and at home. We have more impact, are more effective parents, and we can even be better spouses. We can't learn every habit and belief all at once, but by rereading this book, using video, reflecting, and practicing, we can truly, significantly improve the quality of our lives and even the lives of those around us. I'm going to be working at my conversations, and hope you will too. Together, we can make this world a better place to have a conversation.

Getting Better at Building Trust

To get better at building trust, we need to clarify what we mean by trust, identify our strengths, and make plans to improve in areas that we target. The following forms are intended to help with that reflection and growth.

The *Looking Back: Building Trust* form is designed to help you consider trust in your life by writing about trustworthy and untrustworthy people you have known and by prompting you to make decisions about how you can become more trustworthy.

The *Looking At: Building Trust* form is designed to help you analyze trust and the absence of trust when you experience them. The form is to be used as you watch a movie or show or read a book. Like many of the other reflection forms in this book, this form can be used by one person alone or with a group, but it is especially interesting to use with a group.

The *Looking Ahead: Building Trust* form can be used to help you plan to implement the factors that influence trust—character, competence, reliability, warmth, and stewardship.

TO SUM UP

Any healthy organization or relationship must be built on trust, and several authors have shared different definitions of what trust is. We identify five factors.

- **Character.** We trust someone when we know they won't do us harm. So, to build trust, we must be honest and transparent. When we hold back information or we lie, we demonstrate that we can't be trusted.
- **Reliability.** People trust us when we do what we said we would do when we said we would do it. For that reason, we have to be careful not to overcommit. We can keep enough time to do what we need to do reliably by underpromising and overdelivering, saying no, and using organizational rituals.

- **Competence.** Promises don't mean much unless we can deliver, and trust develops or is diminished depending on how well we do the work that we do. We can increase our competence by developing skills, gaining knowledge, or by being credible.
- **Warmth.** Another way to encourage others to feel safe and trust us is through personal warmth. We can show warmth in the authentic way we listen, demonstrate empathy, share positive information, and be vulnerable.
- **Stewardship.** The more people are focused on themselves, the less we trust them. However, the more people are committed to serving others, the more we trust them. Stewardship is embodied in a genuine focus on others, the way we communicate, the way we give credit to others, and the simple fact that we care.

GOING DEEPER

Megan Tschannen-Moran's book *Trust Matters: Leadership for Successful Schools* (2014) provides excellent information for anyone interested in building trust in schools—and shouldn't that be all of us? Tschannen-Moran includes cases, references recent research, and provides a comprehensive set of definitions and strategies that should help anyone build trust in their schools and homes. This book, along with *Trust in Schools: A Core Resource for Improvement* (2002) by Anthony Bryk and Barbara Schneider, laid the groundwork for much that is being written about trust in education today.

Henry Cloud's *Integrity: The Courage to Meet the Demands of Reality* (2006) is a wise book that provides excellent suggestions on how to build trust—particularly if you hold a leadership position. Cloud's book also discusses five other character dimensions that are essential for leading with integrity. I have reviewed the book a few times as I've written different documents, and I find it to be wise and helpful.

Stephen R. Covey's *The Speed of Trust: The One Thing That Changes Everything* (2006) is a classic work on the topic of this chapter. Covey's book is very helpful for making the case for and defining trust, and I guarantee that if you read what Covey has to say about the 13 trust behaviors, you will learn a lot about how you can be more trustworthy.

LOOKING BACK:

Building Trust

Who is someone that you really trust? What is it that makes them trustworthy?

....

....

....

....

....

Who is someone you do not trust? What is it that makes them untrustworthy?

....

....

....

....

....

Given what you've said above, is there anything you think you should do differently to be more trustworthy?

....

....

....

....

....

Available for download at **http://resources.corwin.com/KnightBetterConversations**

LOOKING AT:

Building Trust

Use this form while watching a film or television program, or reading a novel, that has trustworthy and untrustworthy characters.

List all the ways the filmmaker or author depicts the trustworthy and untrustworthy characters.

TRUSTWORTHY	UNTRUSTWORTHY

Given what you noticed in the film, book, or program, is there anything you think you should do differently to be perceived as more trustworthy?

LOOKING AHEAD:

Building Trust

///

Use this form to consider the factors that influence trust—
character, competence, reliability, warmth, and stewardship.
Identify any changes you can make to become more trustworthy.

CHARACTER

Are you honest, transparent, and nonjudgmental? Do you need to
change so that you can be more trustworthy?

....

....

....

COMPETENCE

How can you increase the usefulness of what you share? Do you need
to be more focused or precise? Do you need to increase your depth of
knowledge?

....

....

....

RELIABILITY

What organizational rituals and boundaries can you add, or what
activities can you quit so you can be more reliable?

....

....

....

WARMTH

Do you need to get better at demonstrating empathy, listening,
being a witness to the good, or being vulnerable to encourage trust?

....

....

....

STEWARDSHIP

Do you need to change your outlook on life in any way so that you
are less concerned with yourself and more concerned with others?

....

....

....

REFERENCES

Allen, J. (2006). *As a man thinketh*. Radford, VA: Wilder Publications.

Angelou, M. (1991). *I shall not be moved*. New York, NY: Random House.

Argyris, C., Putnam, R., & Smith, D. (1985). *Action science*. San Francisco, CA: Jossey Bass.

Berger, W. (2014). *A more beautiful question: The power of inquiry to spark breakthrough ideas*. New York, NY: Bloomsbury USA.

Bernstein, R. J. (1983). *Beyond objectivism and relativism: Science, hermeneutics, and praxis*. Philadelphia, PA: University of Pennsylvania Press.

Block, P. (1993). *Stewardship: Choosing service over self-interest*. San Francisco, CA: Berrett-Koehler.

Bohm, D. (1996). *On dialogue*. Lee Nichol (Ed.). New York, NY: Routledge.

Brown, B. (2010). *The gifts of imperfection: Let go of who you're supposed to be and embrace who you are*. Center City, MN: Hazelden.

Brown, B. (2012). *Daring greatly: How the courage to be vulnerable transforms the way we live, love, parent and lead*. New York, NY: Random House.

Bryk, A., & Schneider, B. (2002). *Trust in schools: A core resource for improvement*. New York, NY: Russell Sage Foundation.

Buber, M. (1970). *I and thou*. New York, NY: Walter Kaufmann.

Buckingham, M., & Coffman, C. (1999). *First break all the rules: What the world's greatest managers do differently*. New York, NY: Simon and Schuster.

Carnegie, D. (1936). *How to win friends and influence people*. New York, NY: Simon & Schuster.

Cloud, H. (2009). *Integrity: The courage to meet the demands of reality*. New York, NY: HarperCollins.

Copen, C. E., Daniels, K., Vespa, J., & Mosher, W. D. (2012). First marriages in the United States: Data from the 2006–2010 national survey of family growth. *National Health Statistics Report, 49*. Hyattsville, MD: National Center for Health Statistics.

Covey, S. (1989). *The 7 habits of highly effective people: Powerful lessons in personal change*. New York, NY: Simon & Schuster.

Covey, S. (2006). *The speed of trust: The one thing that changes everything.* New York, NY: Simon & Schuster.

Deci, E., & Ryan, R. (1995). *Why we do what we do: Understanding self-motivation.* New York, NY: Penguin.

Duhigg, C. (2012). *Power of habits: Why we do what we do in life and business.* New York, NY: Random House.

Dweck, C. S. (2006). *Mindset: The new psychology of success.* New York, NY: Random House.

Ekman, P. (2007). *Emotions revealed: Recognizing faces and feelings to improve communication and emotional life* (2nd ed.). New York, NY: Henry Holt.

Evans, S., & Cohen, S. S. (2000). *Hot buttons: How to resolve conflict and cool everyone down.* New York, NY: HarperCollins.

Fay, J., & Funk, D. (2001). *Love and logic teacherisms: Wise words for teachers.* Golden, CO: Love and Logic.

Fay, J., & Funk, D. (2010). *Teaching with love and logic: Taking control of the classroom.* Golden, CO: Love and Logic.

Fisher, R., & Shapiro, D. (2005). *Beyond reason: Using emotions as you negotiate.* New York, NY: Viking Press.

Fisher, R., Ury, W., & Patton, B. (1991). *Getting to yes: Negotiating agreement without giving in.* New York, NY: Penguin.

Freire, P. (1970). *Pedagogy of the oppressed.* New York, NY: Continuum.

Fullan, M. (2001). *Leading in a culture of change: Being effective in complex times.* San Francisco, CA: Jossey-Bass.

Fullan, M. (2008). *Six secrets of change: What the best leaders do to help their organizations survive and thrive.* San Francisco, CA: Jossey-Bass.

Gadotti, M. (1994). *Reading Freire: His life and work.* Albany, NY: State University of New York Press.

Gallagher, W. (2009). *Rapt: Attention and the focused life.* New York, NY: Penguin.

Gallwey, W. (2001). *The inner game of work: Focus, learning, pleasure and mobility in the workplace.* New York, NY: Random House.

Goldsmith, M. (2007). *What got you here won't get you there: How successful people get even more successful.* New York, NY: HarperCollins.

Goleman, D. (2007). *Social intelligence: The new science of human relationships.* New York, NY: Random House.

Gottman, J. M., & DeClaire, J. (2001). *The relationship cure: A 5 step guide to strengthening your marriage, family, and friendship.* New York, NY: Crown.

Gottman, J. M., Gottman, J. S., & DeClaire, J. (2006). *Ten lessons to transform your marriage: America's love lab experts share their strategies for strengthening your relationship.* New York, NY: Random House.

Gottman, J. M., & Silver, N. (1999). *The seven principles for making marriage work.* New York, NY: Crown.

Greg, A. (Interviewer). (2009). Jeremy Rifkin. *The Empathic Civilization* [video podcast]. Retrieved from http://itunes .apple.com

Hallowell, E. M. (2011). *Shine: Using brain science to get the best from your people.* Boston, MA: Harvard Business School.

Halvorson, H. G. (2015). *No one understands you and what to do about it.* Watertown, MA: Harvard Business Review Press.

Heath, C., & Heath, D. (2007). *Made to stick: Why some ideas survive and others die.* New York, NY: Random House.

Heath, C., & Heath, D. (2013). *Decisive: How to make better choices in life and work.* New York, NY: Random House.

Horn, S. (1996). *Tongue fu: How to deflect, disarm and defuse any conflict.* New York, NY: St. Martin's Press.

Horton, M., & Freire, P. (2010). *We make the road by walking: Conversations on education and social change.* B. Bell, J. Gaventa, & J. Peters (Eds.). Philadelphia, PA: Temple University Press.

Isaacs, W. (1999). *Dialogue and the art of thinking together.* New York, NY: Doubleday.

Kegan, R., & Lahey, L. (2001). *How the way we talk can change the way we learn.* San Francisco, CA: Jossey-Bass.

Kierkegaard, S. (1964). *Purity of heart is to will one thing: Spiritual preparation for the office of confession.* New York, NY: Harper & Row.

Killion, J., & Todnem, G. R. (1991). A process of personal theory building. *Educational Leadership, 48*(2), 14–16.

Knight, J. (2007). *Instructional coaching: A partnership approach to improving instruction.* Thousand Oaks, CA: Corwin.

Knight, J. (2011). *Unmistakable impact: A partnership approach for dramatically improving instruction.* Thousand Oaks, CA: Corwin.

Knight, J. (2014). *Focus on teaching: Using video for high-impact instruction.* Thousand Oaks, CA: Corwin.

Kolb, D. M., & Williams, J. (2000). *The shadow negotiation: How women can master the hidden agendas that determine bargaining success.* San Francisco, CA: Jossey-Bass.

Krznaric, R. (2014). *Empathy: Why it matters, and how to get it.* New York, NY: Penguin.

Loehr, J. S., & Schwartz, T. (2003). *The power of full engagement: Managing energy, not time, is the key to high performance and personal renewal.* New York, NY: Free Press.

Lopez, S. (2013). *Making hope happen: Create the future you want for yourself and others.* New York, NY: Atria Books.

Maister, D. H., Green, C. H., & Galford, R. M. (2000). *The trusted advisor.* New York, NY: Simon & Schuster.

May, M. E. (2007). *The elegant solution: Toyota's formula for mastering innovation.* New York, NY: Simon & Schuster.

Miller, W. R., & Rollnick, S. (2002). *Motivational interviewing: Preparing people for change* (2nd ed.). New York, NY: Guilford Press.

Nepo, M. (2013). *Seven thousand ways to listen: Staying close to what is sacred*. New York, NY: Simon & Schuster.

Nietzsche, F. (1966). *Beyond good and evil: Prelude to a philosophy of the future*. W. Kaufman (Ed.). Mineola, NY: Dover.

Nonaka, I., & Takeuchi, H. (1995). *The knowledge creating company: How Japanese companies create the dynamics of innovation*. New York, NY: Oxford University Press.

Oxford English Dictionary (7th ed.) (2012). Cory, NC: Oxford University Press.

Palmer, P. (2011). *Healing the heart of democracy: The courage to create a politics of the human spirit*. San Francisco, CA: Jossey-Bass.

Palmer, P. J. (2007). *The courage to teach: Exploring the inner landscape of a teacher's life* (10th ed.). San Francisco, CA: Jossey-Bass.

Palmer, P. J. (2009). *A hidden wholeness: The journey toward an undivided life*. San Francisco, CA: Jossey-Bass.

Patterson, K., Grenny, J., McMillan, R., & Switzler, A. (2002). *Crucial conversations: Tools for talking when stakes are high*. New York, NY: McGraw-Hill.

Polanyi, M. (1958). *Personal knowledge*. Chicago, IL: University of Chicago Press.

Purkey, W., & Novak, J. M. (n.d.). "Forty Inviting Comments" and "Forty Disinviting Comments." Retrieved from http://www.mysdcc.sdccd.edu/Staff/Instructor_Development/Content/HTML/Forty_Successes.htm

Quaglia, J., & Corso, M. J. (2014). *Student voice: The instrument of change*. Thousand Oaks, CA: Corwin.

Reina, D. S., & Reina, M. L. (2006). *Trust and betrayal in the workplace: Building effective relationships in your organization* (2nd ed.). San Francisco, CA: Berrett-Koehler.

Rifkin, J. (2009). *The empathic civilization: The race to global consciousness in a world in crisis*. New York, NY: Penguin.

Roberts, M. (1997). *The man who listens to horses*. New York, NY: Random House.

Rosenberg, M. B. (2003). *Nonviolent communication: A language of life*. Encenitas, CA: Puddle Dancer Press.

Rothstein, D., & Santana, L. (2011). *Make just one change: Teach students to ask their own questions*. Cambridge, MA: Harvard Education Press.

Ruiz, D. M. (1997). *The four agreements: A practical guide to personal freedom*. San Rafael, CA: Amber-Allen.

Schein, E. H. (2009). *Helping: How to offer, give, and receive help*. San Francisco, CA: Berrett-Koehler.

Schein, E. H. (2010). *Organizational culture and leadership*. San Francisco, CA: Jossey-Bass.

Schein, E. H. (2013). *Humble inquiry: The gentle art of asking instead of telling*. San Francisco, CA: Berrett-Koehler.

Schlechty, P. (2011). *Engaging students: The next level of working on the work*. San Francisco, CA: Jossey-Bass.

Schön, D. A. (1991). *The reflective turn: Case studies in and on educational practice*. New York, NY: Teachers Press, Columbia University.

Scott, S. (2002). *Fierce conversations: Achieving success at work and in life, one conversation at a time*. New York, NY: Penguin.

Seligman, M. (1998). *Learned optimism: How to change your mind and your life*. New York, NY: Simon & Schuster.

Seligman, M. (2006). *Learned optimism: How to change your mind and your life*. New York, NY: Simon & Schuster.

Seligman, M. (2011). *Flourish: A visionary new understanding of happiness and well-being*. New York, NY: Simon & Schuster.

Senge, P. (2006). *The fifth discipline: The art and practice of the learning organization*. London, UK: Random House.

Steckel, R., & Steckel, M. (2010). *Milestones project*. Retrieved from http://milestonesproject.com

Stoltzfus, T. (2008). *Coaching questions: A coach's guide to powerful asking skills*. Charleston, SC: Book Surge.

Stone, R. (1996). *The healing art of storytelling: A sacred journey of personal discovery*. New York, NY: Hyperion.

Stone, D., Patton, B., Heen, S., & Fisher, R. (2000). *Difficult conversations: How to discuss what matters most*. New York, NY: Penguin.

Sutton, R. (2010). *Good boss bad boss: How to be the best . . . and learn from the worst*. New York, NY: Hachette Book Group.

Tschannen-Moran, M. (2014). *Trust matters: Leadership for successful schools* (2nd ed.). San Francisco, CA: Jossey-Bass.

Tutu, D. (2000). *No future without forgiveness*. New York, NY: Doubleday.

Ury, W. (1993). *Getting past no: Negotiating your way from confrontation to cooperation*. New York, NY: Bantam Books.

Wheatley, M. J. (2002). *Turning to one another: Simple conversations to restore hope to the future*. San Francisco, CA: Berrett-Koehler.

Wiggins, G. (2014, October 10). A veteran teacher turned coach shadows two students for two days: A sobering lesson learned. [Web log post]. Retrieved from https://grantwiggins.wordpress.com/2014/10/10/a-veteran-teacher-turned-coach-shadows-2-students-for-2-days-a-sobering-lesson-learned/

Yankelovich, D. (1999). *The magic of dialogue: Transforming conflict into cooperation*. New York, NY: Simon & Schuster.

Zalta, E. N. (Ed.). (2015). *The Stanford encyclopedia of philosophy*. Stanford, CA: The Metaphysics Lab, Stanford University.

Zeldin, T. (1998). *Conversation: How talk can change our lives*. Mahwah, NJ: HiddenSpring.

STUDY PARTICIPANTS

Sarah Aguilar
Marilyn Allen
Janet Attallah
Marisol Audia
Lisl Bahrynowski
Stephanie Barnhill
Helen Barrier
Lisa Benham
Deborah Bidulka
Jittinun Boonsathirakul
Cathy Booth
Dan Breyfogle
Andrea Broomell
Laura Browder
Gretchen Brown
Patty Brus
Jennifer Bush
Janette Cochran
Ben Collins
Stacie Collins
Bev Columbo
Ann Compton
Katie Cooke
Dympna Cybulski
Karin Cyganov
Corina DeGuire
Juliana Dempsey
Jenni Donohoo
Julia Drefs
Chelle Dunham
Allison Duty
Moly Edelen

Sherry Eichenger
Susan Ellison
Carol Fancher
Sarah Fitzsimmons
Rhonda Fode
Todd Fornadel
LuAnn Fountaine
Maira Furgiuele
Sue Gallagher
Sandra Gearhart
Alex Geddes
Michellle Gilbert
Wendy Grimm
Mon Grof
Candace Hall
Tony Harmon
Michelle Harris
Anne Highfield
Norah Hooper
Susan Hope
Steve Houqwen
Paige Fenton Hughes
Jenny Jacobs
Shawn Johnson
Alissa Jones
Jim Justice
Kendra Kanzlik
Debbie Kessler
Paula Keyack
Stephanie Kilchenstein
Joellen Killion
Keli Kinsella

Jolene Kovechne
Ron Lalonde
Joy Lang
Beth Lasky
Sherri Latigna
Linda Lawrey
Lisa Lee
Linda Leggett
Mary Liebl
Kristie Lofland
Beth Madison
Emily Manning
Carolyn Matteson
Carol McBroom
Debra McCain
Karen McCollum
Martha Moore
Vicki Moras
Margaret Morgan
Michelle Murray
Lindsey Myers
Greg Netzer
Brent Okrainetz
Shana Olson
Lisa Onkotz
DeWayne Padgett
Sarah Pankonien
Nicole Patton
Cynthia Paul
Lori Pearson
Emily Peterson
Pona Piearski
Ruth Poage
Mindi Polanski
Linda Reetz
Sue Renehan

Karen Ruhs
Donna Rush
Amy Russell
Kathy Sadler
Lou Sangdahl
Patty Sankey
Sida Scharff
Christine Schneiders
Andrea Shaw
Lisa Sligh
Chris Slocum
Deb Smith
Deidre Smith
Joel Smith
Adlyn Soellner
Michael Soguero
Jennifer Solomon
Joel Solomon
Lynn Stack
Amy Stadum
Jennifer Stadum
Amy Stephenson
Barbara Stolarik
Karen Taylor
Phil Taylor
Bonnie Tomberlyn
Courtney Tuck
Carol Walker
Jill Walker
Jocelyn Washburn
Kim Watchhorn
Kris Weingaetner-Hartke
Kendra Williams
Lisa Williams
Carol Wolf

INDEX

CORWIN

A SAGE Company

Helping educators make the greatest impact

CORWIN HAS ONE MISSION: to enhance education through intentional professional learning.

We build long-term relationships with our authors, educators, clients, and associations who partner with us to develop and continuously improve the best evidence-based practices that establish and support lifelong learning.

Solutions you want. Experts you trust. Results you need.

AUTHOR CONSULTING

Author Consulting

On-site professional learning with sustainable results! Let us help you design a professional learning plan to meet the unique needs of your school or district. www.corwin.com/pd

INSTITUTES

Institutes

Corwin Institutes provide collaborative learning experiences that equip your team with tools and action plans ready for immediate implementation. www.corwin.com/institutes

ECOURSES

eCourses

Practical, flexible online professional learning designed to let you go at your own pace. www.corwin.com/ecourses

READ2EARN

Read2Earn

Did you know you can earn graduate credit for reading this book? Find out how: www.corwin.com/read2earn

Contact an account manager at (800) 831-6640 or visit **www.corwin.com** for more information.